THE HUNTING & FISHING LIBRARY®

FISHING WITH LIVE BAIT

By Dick Sternberg

DICK STERNBERG is widely recognized as an expert fisherman and outdoor writer. Dick was a professional fisheries biologist for 16 years.

CREDITS:
Project Director and Author: Dick Sternberg
Editorial Director: Chuck Wechsler
Design and Production: Cy DeCosse Creative Department, Inc.
Art Directors: Cy DeCosse, Delores Swanson
Production Coordinators: Mary Ann Knox, Christine Watkins
Staff Photographers: Graham Brown, Buck Holzemer, Michael Jensen, Bill Lindner, Steven McHugh, Doug Stamm
Staff Researchers/Writers: Joel Bich, Joseph Cella, Jay Strangis
Production Staff: Michelle Alexander, Brian Berkey, Diane Johnson, Ann Mackey, Bernice Maehren, Jennie Smith, Ellen Sorenson, Elizabeth Woods
Contributing Photographers: Erwin and Peggy Bauer, Brian Berkey, Cy DeCosse, Charley Dickey, Patricia D. Duncan, Dr. Calvin R. Fremling, David Hall, Robert L. Jeanne, Robert J. R. Johnson, David Kumlien, Steve Munson, Nebraska Game & Parks Commission, M. Timothy O'Keefe, Don Oster, C. Boyd Pfeiffer, Allan J. Ristori, Jerry Robb, William Roston, Frank Sargeant, Dr. William D. Schmid, Bill Scifres, Richard P. Smith, J. D. Solomon, Dick Sternberg, James Tallon, Virginia A. Vail, Dr. Thomas F. Waters, Chuck Wechsler, C. Herb Williams, Dr. Thomas H. Wilson
Illustrator: Don Hannum
Special Consultant: Joe Ehrhardt
Consultants: Willie Breese, Oregon State University; Max Bachhuber, Bantas Fishing Float; Edwin F. Cook, Dr. Donald Gilbertson, Dr. Thomas F. Waters, University of Minnesota; Kay Etheridge, University of Florida-Gainesville; Butch Furtman; Carl Lowrance; Bill Plaia, Virginia A. Vail, Scott Willis, Florida Department of Natural Resources; Bill Schieman; Dr. Thomas H. Wilson, Judson College; Herb Williams
Cooperating Agencies and Individuals: Alumacraft Boat Co.; B. H. Electronics, Inc.; Dan Bailey, Rainbow Plastics, Inc.; Dan Bailey Flies & Tackle; Bill Binkelman; Harold Blaisdell; Lyndon Bond, Robert Foye, Maine Department of Inland Fisheries and Wildlife; Don Bonneau, Iowa State Conservation Commission; Bob Buda; Burger Brothers; Tony Burmek; Horace Carter; Mike Chamberlain, Ted's Sports Center; Fred Cibik; Dr. Hollie L. Collins, University of Minnesota-Duluth; Dr. James Cox, Cox Family Laboratories, Inc.; Dr. Whitney Cranshaw, Rod Kuehn, University of Minnesota; George Day III, The Day Bait Co.; Margie F. Duescher, VMC, Inc.; Dan Dygert, Swamp Creek Crawfish Company; Melida Evans, Evans Bait and Tackle; E-Z Loader Boat Trailers; Mike Fennel; Float-Hi Balsa Float Co.; John Foster, Maryland Department of Natural Resources; Dr.

Calvin R. Fremling, Winona State University; Dan D. Gapen, Gapen's World of Fishing; Larry Gates, Howard Krosch, Mike Mueller, Dirk Peterson, Duane Shodeen, Minnesota Department of Natural Resources; Mitch Gilbert; Robert Graves, Tropical Fish Farm, Ltd.; Marvin Guffey, G & S Wholesale Bait; Frank Haw, Washington State Department of Fisheries; Hub's Bait & Tackle; Robin Jensen, Capitol Tackle, Inc.; Daryl Karns; Jack Kearney, Brown Bear Bait, Inc.; Jack Kenyon, Grand Lake Tackle Co.; Klaus Kjelstrup, O. Mustad and Son, Inc.; Leroy Knutson, Knute's Bait Shop; David Kumlien, Wild Wings Orvis Shop; Larry Larsen; Ron Linder; George Lobough, Mohave Valley News; Lowrance Electronics; Lowrance Waterdog Farms; Terrance Majure, Mississippi Department of Wildlife Conservation; Mariner Outboards; Dave Martin, Sportsmans Taxidermy and Natural Baits; Vern McPherson, Mack's Lure Manufacturing Co., Inc.; Mercury Outboards; Meter Fishing Tackle; Floyd Moser; George Nace, University of Michigan; Mike Nascak, Lakeside Bait; Bruce Nelson, Goldeneye Products, Inc.; Buddy Nordmann; Plastilite Corp.; Michael Plummer, Harding University; Darrell Raffety, Raffety's Fish Bait; Buzz Ramsey, Luhr Jensen and Sons, Inc.; Sam E. Rayburn, Western Tackle and Manufacturing; Allan J. Ristori; Roy's Bait; Bill Scifres; Jim Slebiska; Lindy Stoltz; Lee Strait, British Columbia Ministry of Environment Environmental Management Division; Norm Strung; Allan Tarvid; Craig Treat; Greg Trouth, Wright and McGill Co.; University of Minnesota Landscape Arboretum; Gary VanderMause, Uncle Josh Bait Co.; Vexilar, Inc.; Tom Walters, The Ontario Federation of Anglers and Hunters; Water Gremlin; Dwight Wilcox, Ojibway Bait Co.; Susie Williamson, Smitty's Bait and Tackle
Color Separations: Weston Engraving Co., Inc.
Printing: Times Offset Pte Ltd, Singapore (0490)

Also available from the publisher: *The Art of Freshwater Fishing, Cleaning & Cooking Fish, Largemouth Bass, Panfish, The Art of Hunting, Fishing With Artificial Lures, Walleye, Smallmouth Bass, Dressing & Cooking Wild Game, Freshwater Gamefish of North America, Fishing Update No. 1, Trout, Secrets of the Fishing Pros, Fishing Rivers & Streams*

Contents

Introduction

Over three-fourths of all gamefish caught in the fresh waters of North America are taken on live bait. Even fishermen who favor artificial lures switch to live bait when fish are difficult to catch. They know that an artificial lure cannot duplicate the smell, action and texture of the real thing. In this book, the term live bait includes not only baits that are alive, but also cut-baits, frozen baits and preserved natural baits.

The purpose of this book is to make you a better live-bait fisherman. The first section will help you choose the terminal tackle and other equipment needed for successful live-bait fishing. Following that are sections on baitfish, worms and leeches, insects, salamanders and frogs, and crustaceans. Also included is information on fishing with salmon eggs, fish parts, preserved baits and even clams. When and where to catch gamefish is discussed briefly, but is covered more thoroughly in other books in The Hunting & Fishing Library.

This book focuses on the most effective live baits and the gamefish for which they work best. Step-by-step photos show how to hook and rig each bait. Most baits can be rigged dozens of different ways. An insect rig recommended for trout may also work when using worms for panfish. Fishermen should experiment to find the hooking and rigging methods that work best in the waters they fish.

A few of the rigs and techniques shown in this book may be illegal in some areas. Many states and provinces also have laws restricting the transportation and use of certain baits. It is illegal to transport live baitfish into Canada. All baitfish are banned in much of the Pacific Northwest to keep undesirable species out of prime fishing waters. Rough fish are prohibited in other areas for the same reason. Other baits are restricted because they are too effective or because their populations are declining. Be sure to check state or provincial fishing regulations.

Catching your own live bait can be almost as much fun as fishing with it. And as expert anglers know, many of the best live baits cannot be purchased at bait shops. You have to catch them yourself. This book contains dozens of photos of live baits in their natural habitats. It outlines their ranges, the season or time of day when they can be collected most easily, and other tips to help you find them. Featured are the most effective methods and gear for capturing live bait, including many homemade traps and collecting devices that work as well as anything purchased at a sporting goods store.

Whether you catch your own bait or buy it at a bait shop, you should know how to keep it fresh and lively. Fish are more apt to strike a bait that is in good condition. And, you can save money by keeping your bait alive. This book shows you the best ways of keeping each type of bait, for a one-day fishing trip or for extended periods.

Most fishermen stick with baits and rigs that have produced in the past. They switch only after the proven methods fail. But by that time, fish have usually quit biting. So, when the new baits fail to catch fish, few anglers will try them again — that's human nature. When testing a new bait, hook it on to start the day and give it a fair trial. You may just discover that it works better than the old standbys.

Equipment for Live-bait Fishing

Natural bait demands more fishing finesse than artificial lures. A big bass may instinctively chase a fast-moving lure, but a fish usually has more time to inspect natural bait.

To present live bait naturally, fishermen must use the right type of line and terminal tackle. If the line is too visible or the hook too big, a gamefish will ignore even the most appetizing bait. If the sinker is too heavy or the float too large, a fish will feel too much resistance and quickly drop the bait.

Fishermen should also select the right rod and reel for the task. Casting a tiny insect may require an ultralight spinning outfit, but heaving a one-pound baitfish demands heavy-duty bait-casting gear. A long cane pole works best for lowering a worm into a small pocket in thick weeds.

Most live-bait fishermen use clear monofilament line because it is least visible to fish. Thin-diameter, flexible mono enables anglers to present bait naturally. You can land a heavy fish on light line, but it takes extra time. Light line is not practical for fishing in thick cover or snaggy bottoms. Heavy monofilament line may spook fish, and its stiffness restricts the action of small baits.

When fishing in rocks or snags, use a hard-finish line that resists abrasion. It pays to select premium monofilament. It is more durable than cheaper grades and less likely to have weak spots.

Tips for Using Monofilament Line

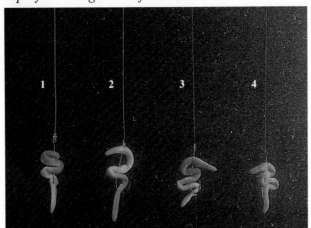

LINE WEIGHT determines its visibility in water. These lines are the same brand and color. (1) 30-pound line is thicker and more visible than (2) 17-pound line, (3) 10-pound or (4) 2-pound line.

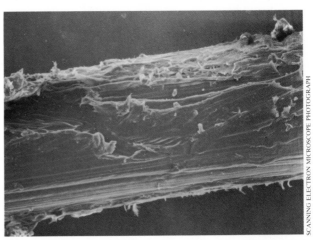

NICKS AND ABRASIONS can be seen in this photo of line magnified 80 times. Run the line between your fingers. If you feel a rough spot, cut the line and retie the hook. Tug on the line periodically to make sure it is strong.

Hooks

A hook is the least expensive item in a tackle box but probably the most important. Experienced anglers consider many factors when selecting a hook.

Hook size is determined by the size of the fish's mouth and the bait. To catch fish, the hook must be large enough so the point protrudes slightly from the bait. Fish may ignore the bait if the point or shank is too visible. Use a hook no longer than needed for the bait and method of hooking.

Wire thickness depends on the size of the bait and bottom conditions. A light-wire hook works best for small baits such as insects; a heavy-wire hook would damage them. A light-wire hook may straighten enough to pull free when snagged but it could also straighten while you fight a large fish. Most anglers use heavy-wire hooks for large, hard-fighting fish.

The finish of a hook can be important but is largely a matter of personal preference. Most bait hooks have a bronze finish, which is inexpensive but rusts quickly. Nickel, cadmium, Perma Plate® and stainless steel hooks are corrosion-resistant. Some fishermen believe that silver or gold-colored hooks attract more fish. Green hooks are least visible under water. Hooks also come in blued and black finishes.

Other considerations when choosing a hook include length and shape of the point, position of the eye, and hardness. Hooks come in a variety of styles. Choose the style best suited to your type of fishing.

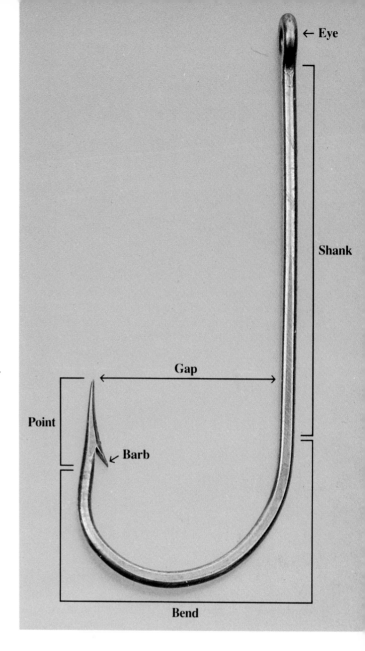

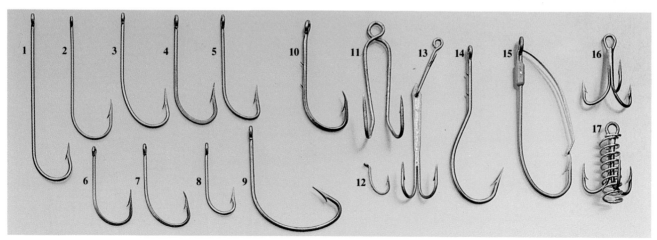

HOOK STYLES for live-bait fishing include: (1) Carlisle, (2) Aberdeen, (3) Sproat, (4) O'Shaughnessy, (5) Limerick, (6) National Round, Round Bend or Viking, (7) Faultless, Claw or Beak, (8) Kirby, (9) Wide Gap, Wide Bend or Kahle®, (10) sliced-shank Baitholder hook, (11) Super Hook®, (12) egg hook, (13) double-needle hook, (14) plastic-worm hook, (15) weedless hook, (16) treble hook, (17) Soft Bait Treble.

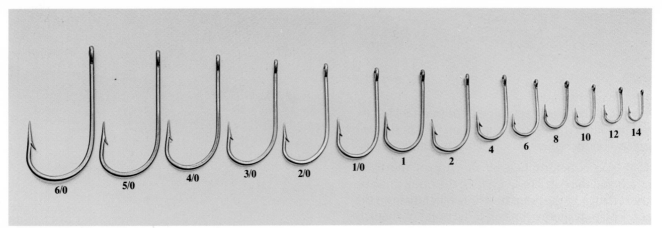

SIZE is designated by a number which reflects the *gap*, or distance between the point and the inside of the shank. Manufacturers produce a full range of sizes for each style. Larger hooks, from 1/0 to 6/0, increase in size as the number increases. But smaller hooks, from #1 to #14, decrease in size as the number increases. Hooks come in larger and smaller sizes, but these are the most commonly used. Shown are actual size VMC National Rounds.

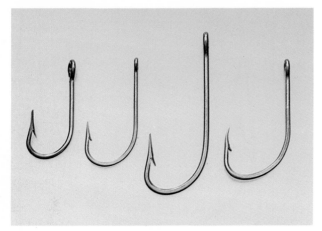

GAP varies from one hook style to another. Shown are four styles of 3/0 hooks from the same manufacturer. Each has a different gap size. To further complicate the matter, different manufacturers may produce the same hook style and size with different gaps.

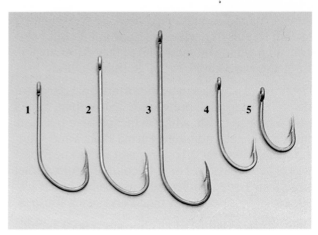

SHANKS are available in different lengths in the same style. A Claw hook is produced in a (1) standard length, but is also made in (2) long and (3) extra-long shanks. An O'Shaughnessy hook is produced in (4) standard length and (5) short shank.

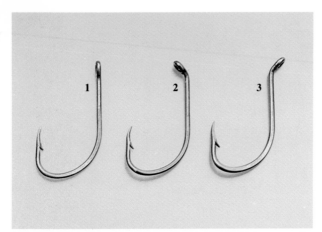

EYE POSITION is (1) straight, or *ringed*, on most bait hooks. Some fishermen claim that a (2) *turned-down* eye is better for hooking because it directs the point into the fish. (3) A *turned-up* eye is often used for snelling.

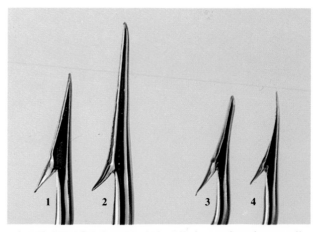

POINT LENGTH AND SHAPE determines how well a hook penetrates and holds. (1) A short point sinks easily; (2) a long point holds better. (3) A spear point is stronger; (4) a hollow point is thinner and penetrates better.

Sharpening Hooks

Most fishermen do not bother to sharpen their fish hooks. When a point breaks or becomes dull, they simply tie on a new hook. But a new hook is not necessarily a sharp hook.

Cheap hooks are usually made of soft, low-grade steel and are poorly sharpened. Even a new, high-quality hook dulls quickly, or the tip of the point bends or breaks when dragged over rocks or through debris. Examine your hook frequently to see if it needs sharpening.

Many anglers carry honing stones or flat files in their tackle boxes for touching up hook points. The usual sharpening method is to hone the point to a round, conical shape. Do not make the point too thin because it may break when setting the hook into a hard-mouthed fish.

A method that is becoming more popular is called *triangular sharpening.* A point with three cutting edges penetrates better than a cone-shaped point.

SHARP POINTS penetrate better and catch more fish than dull ones. These hooks, magnified 15 times actual size, include (top to bottom): a new hook, a hook that has been fished on a rocky bottom and a hook sharpened by the triangular sharpening method.

The Triangular Sharpening Method

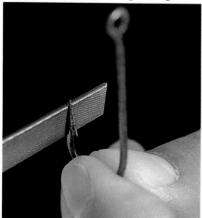 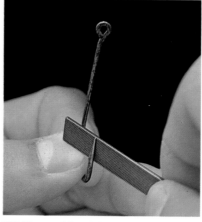 

FLATTEN the outside edge of the point using a hook file. Begin filing at the barb and work toward the point of the hook.

FILE one side of the point, beginning at the barb. Remove enough metal so the side is flat and slanted toward the inside of the point.

TURN the hook and file the other side of the point in the same manner. When completed, the point should be three-sided.

Bobbers

Called a bobber, float or cork, this simple device serves several important functions. It provides extra weight for casting light baits, suspends the bait where fish are feeding and signals a bite.

When selecting a bobber, take into account the size of the bait, the depth of fish, and how well the float can be seen by you and the fish.

A 1-inch round plastic bobber will easily float a small fathead minnow, but a 10-inch sucker will pull the bobber under and swim away with it. Experi-enced anglers carry a variety of sizes, and choose the smallest bobber that will still hold up the bait.

Fishermen use two types of bobbers: *fixed* and *sliding*. Fixed bobbers work well when fish are no deeper than a rod length. When fishing deeper water, casting is difficult because of the long length of line between the bobber and bait. To suspend a bait in deep water, thread on a slip-bobber or sliding float. Because the float slides, it can be reeled almost to the rod tip. Once cast, the bobber floats on the surface while the line slips through until stopped by a knot that holds the bait at the desired depth.

Fish in clear, shallow water can easily see a floating object. Many anglers use transparent plastic bub-bles for casting tiny baits to stream trout. When fishing deep, murky or choppy water, use a bobber that is highly visible. Bright-colored floats that stand high above the surface are easier to see than low-profile floats.

BALANCE your bobber carefully. Add enough split-shot so the bobber floats just high enough to be seen. An improperly balanced bobber (right) is harder to pull under and may cause the fish to drop the bait.

SELECT a float that is easy to see. A fluorescent cylinder float (left) stands out on a rippled surface much better than a round, white clip-bobber (right). Use a lighted bobber when fishing at night.

KEEP your slip-bobber close to the boat (left) when fishing in deep water. Anchor near the fishing spot and lower the line over the side. This way, you can set the hook with a direct pull. Avoid casting the slip-bobber too

far from the boat (right). When the bait sinks into deep water, the float creates a right angle in the line between you and the bait. Then, it is nearly impossible to set the hook because you do not have a straight-line pull.

SLIDING BOBBERS include: (1) cylinder float, (2) slot bobber with wire line-stays, (3) tube bobber, (4) slot bobber with plastic tab line-stays, (5) lighted bobber powered by a lithium battery, (6) Carbonyte® float.

FIXED BOBBERS include: (7) quill float, (8) spring-lock bobber, (9) and (10) casting bubbles, (11) sponge bobber for ice fishing, (12) clip-bobber, (13) Carolina Float®, (14) weighted casting float, (15) peg bobber.

Sinkers

SLIDING SINKERS include: (1) walking sinker, (2) Snap-Loc™ sinker which clips on the line for changing weights easily, (3) cone sinker for retrieving baits through weeds, (4) egg sinker.

Some sinkers attach to the line; others slide on the line. Attached or fixed sinkers are pinched, twisted or tied onto the line. When a fish runs, it must tow the sinker along. Sometimes gamefish will not tolerate this added resistance and will drop the bait. Use the lightest fixed sinker that will still carry your bait to the desired depth.

A sliding or slip-sinker lets the fish swim off without feeling any drag. The sinker rests on bottom while the line slides through it. Slip-sinkers will not work when trolling in mid-water or when bobber-fishing. If the sinker cannot rest on bottom, the line will not slip. A slip-sinker rig is more difficult to tie and requires more hardware than a fixed sinker rig.

When selecting a sinker, consider the depth of water, type of bottom and speed at which the bait is pulled through the water. Fishermen generally switch to heavier sinkers as the depth or speed of the bait increases. When trolling, water resistance pushes the line upward, raising the sinker off bottom. The faster you troll, the more weight you need to keep your bait at the same depth. When drifting, a strong wind pushes the boat faster, making a heavier sinker necessary.

If fishing a river, the speed of the current is important. Switch to heavier sinkers as the current speed increases. To keep baits from rolling downstream, use a flat-sided sinker such as a pyramid. When drifting a bait with the current, use a rounded sinker.

If a lake or stream bottom is covered with rocks or other debris, use a bottom-walker or other type of snag-resistant sinker. Some sinkers are designed to pull free of the line when snagged, leaving the remainder of the rig intact.

Tips for Using Sinkers

SELECT a slip-sinker (right) heavy enough to troll on bottom with a short line. Fish cannot detect the weight because the line slips through. With a light sinker, the line trails too far behind, making it hard to detect a bite.

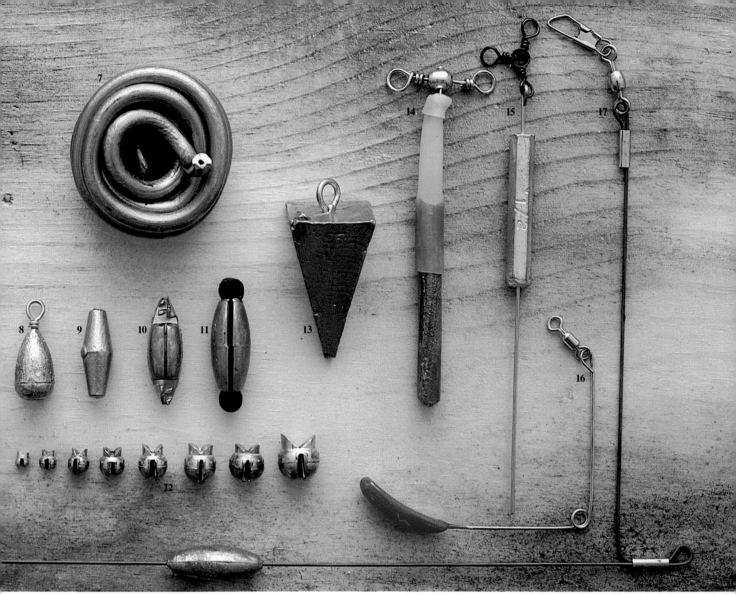

FIXED SINKERS include: (5) keel and (6) torpedo Bead Chain® sinkers to prevent line twist, (7) lead wire which is cut to length and pinched on, (8) bell or dipsey, (9) drift sinker which is pinched on a dropper, (10) pinch-on sinker, (11) Rubbercor®, (12) split-shot in various sizes, (13) pyramid, (14) surgical tubing sinker with lead insert. Bottom-walker types include: (15) Needle Weight™, (16) Bait-Walker™, (17) Bottom Walker™.

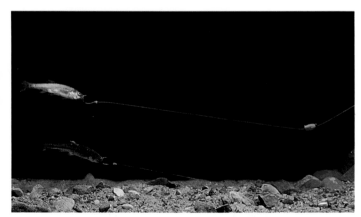

CHOOSE a heavier sinker when using heavier line. Despite identical sinkers, water resistance keeps the 12-pound line (top) from sinking as fast as the 4-pound line, especially when trolled or fished in current.

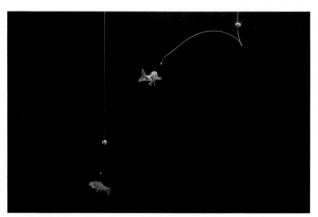

ATTACH the sinker far enough from the bait so it does not interfere with the swimming action. The minnow at left is severely restricted, but the one at right can swim freely, attracting more fish.

Rods and Reels

Horsing a big bass out of thick weeds requires a different rod and reel than needed for casting a tiny insect into a stream riffle. Your rod and reel must suit the bait as well as the fish you hope to catch.

Most live-bait fishermen prefer ultralight to medium-power spinning gear with light monofilament line. In addition to being nearly invisible in water, light mono flows off a fixed-spool reel with almost no friction. This makes it possible to cast extremely light baits with little or no added weight.

Bait fishermen use other types of gear for special purposes. Heavy-duty spinning or surf-casting equipment works best for long casts. Bait-casting tackle is needed for tossing heavy baits. Fly-casting equipment is handy for stream fishing. Even the cane pole is an important bait-fishing tool. It enables fishermen to place baits in spots impossible to reach by casting. Experienced anglers carry two or three different outfits so they are prepared for a variety of fishing situations.

When to Use Spinning Gear

FLIP lures into hard-to-reach spots with a light, flexible spinning rod. A short rod helps you avoid snagging weeds or brush on the backcast.

CAST small baits with light spinning tackle. Most anglers prefer 4- to 6-pound monofilament, but some use 2-pound line for extremely light baits.

When to Use Surf-casting and Bait-casting Gear

DISTANCE CASTING requires a long powerful rod. An 8- to 9-foot surf-casting outfit provides leverage for long casts and holds enough line to handle a big fish.

PULLING fish out of heavy cover demands a stout, powerful, bait-casting rod with at least 20-pound line. A stiff rod also works best for casting heavy baits.

When to Use Fly-casting Gear

FLOAT insects on the surface or keep sinking baits adrift in mid-water by using a fly rod with floating line.

POKE a long fly rod through heavy weeds or brush to reach spots where casting would be difficult.

BOUNCE a bait along bottom with a sensitive fly rod. Keep the rod tip high to detect the slightest bite.

When to Use a Cane Pole

LOWER a delicate bait with a cane, extension or zip pole. Casting may rip out the hook.

REACH several pockets in the weeds without lifting anchor. Moving the boat is likely to disturb the fish.

LIFT fish straight out of heavy weeds before they can dash into cover and tangle your line.

Baitfish

Minnows & Other Baitfish

To most fishermen, the word *minnow* means any small fish used for bait. Technically, minnows are members of a family that includes 250 species in North America. Anglers use many of these for bait, including shiners, chubs, dace, and even goldfish and carp.

The term *baitfish* includes not only minnows, but other fish used by anglers such as suckers, sculpins, madtoms, eels, lampreys and small gamefish.

To be effective, baitfish do not necessarily have to match items in the diets of gamefish. The fathead, a widely-used baitfish, thrives in small ponds but is rarely abundant in lakes or streams with gamefish. Many northern pike fishermen use creek chubs, while some walleye enthusiasts prefer hornyhead chubs. Both minnows are river species and are not found in lakes inhabited by pike and walleyes.

Following are some characteristics of baitfish that determine their effectiveness for catching gamefish:

HARDINESS AND ACTION. These are the most important considerations because nearly all gamefish prefer fresh, lively baits. Although an emerald shiner may look attractive, it may not stay alive long enough to reach your fishing destination, especially during warm weather. Fatheads, on the other hand, can withstand drastic changes in water temperature, low oxygen levels and rough handling. Generally, the hardiest species are liveliest on the hook.

SIZE. When selecting baitfish, choose the size best suited to the fish you expect to catch. Panfishermen often hook on baitfish too large, while pike and catfish anglers use baitfish that are too small. An 8-inch panfish may peck at a 4-inch minnow, but swallowing it is another matter. Large predator fish are lazy. They prefer to eat one large fish rather than many small ones.

SHAPE. Most gamefish prefer long, thin baitfish. Bluegills and other deep-bodied baitfish are difficult to swallow and may lodge in a predator's throat. Fish with big mouths, such as largemouth bass and striped bass, are less selective about shape.

FLASH. Fished side by side, a silvery baitfish will usually catch more fish than a drab one. For this reason, shiners make excellent bait. Ciscoes, smelt, alewives and shad also have silver bodies but are more difficult to keep alive.

TASTE AND SMELL. To find food, catfish rely heavily on taste sensors in and around their whisker-like barbels. Shad, alewives, smelt and other oily baitfish are good catfish baits because they give off a stronger odor than lean-fleshed fish. Other gamefish rely on taste and smell, but to a lesser degree.

SEX. During the breeding season, some male minnows become brightly colored. A few anglers prefer to fish with these colorful males. In some cases, females attract more gamefish. Expert walleye fishermen claim that female fatheads catch more fish than male fatheads. However, with most baitfish, sex is not a factor.

FLASH off silvery shiners is likely to tempt more strikes than the dull appearance of a mudminnow, sucker, chub or other drab baitfish, especially if the water is clear and the sun is shining.

SMELL makes some baitfish more attractive than others that look nearly identical. Walleyes and smallmouth bass are attracted to the scent of a madtom (foreground), but are only moderately interested in the bullhead.

Hardiness Chart

HARDINESS	BAITFISH SPECIES
Extremely Hardy	American eel, mudminnow, fathead minnow, madtom
Moderately Hardy	Blacknose dace, bluegill, bluntnose minnow, creek chub, finescale dace, goldfish, hornyhead chub, mottled sculpin, southern redbelly dace, white sucker
Somewhat Hardy	Banded killifish, common shiner, golden shiner, red shiner, yellow perch
Least Hardy	Alewife, cisco, emerald shiner, gizzard shad, rainbow smelt, spottail shiner

SEX of a baitfish occasionally affects fishing success. Female fatheads (foreground) may be effective because of their lighter color, although some anglers believe male fatheads give off an odor that is objectionable to fish.

How to Identify Minnows

The minnows shown on these pages are some of the most popular bait species. Other, less common species can be equally effective.

GOLDFISH resemble carp. Both have a saw-toothed spine on the dorsal and anal fins, but goldfish lack barbels. Goldfish are found throughout the United States.

FATHEADS, also called *tuffies* or *mudminnows*, have a short first ray on the dorsal fin. They live in lakes and rivers throughout most of North America.

BLUNTNOSE MINNOWS have a more rounded nose than the fathead and a dark band from tail to eye. They live in waters in the eastern half of the United States.

HORNYHEAD CHUBS, or *redtail chubs,* have a lateral band that extends to a tail spot. They prefer gravelly streams from Wyoming to New York, south to Arkansas.

RED SHINERS are deep-bodied and rarely exceed 3 inches. Males have orange fin edges. They are common in large, slow rivers from the Midwest to Mexico.

CREEK CHUBS look similar to the hornyhead chub, but have smaller scales and a dark spot at the front base of the dorsal fin. One of the most common stream minnows in eastern North America, it thrives in waters with gravel bottoms. The creek chub is found east of the Rockies in the United States and southern Canada.

FINESCALE DACE have smaller scales and are less colorful than the redbelly dace. They live in bogs, streams and lakes in the Great Lakes region and parts of Canada.

SOUTHERN REDBELLY DACE, or *rainbows*, have a reddish belly and two dark bands on the side. They are found in the Midwest and South in small streams.

BLACKNOSE DACE have dark blotches on the body and a black line between the eye and nose. They live in fast-water streams in the eastern half of North America.

COMMON SHINERS have a broad body and deep, narrow scales. They live in streams and some lakes from Saskatchewan to Colorado, east to the Atlantic Coast.

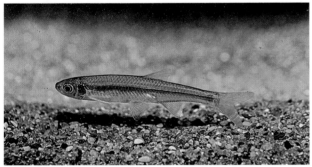

EMERALD SHINERS have a slender body and a large faint band along the side. They thrive in lakes and rivers in the eastern two-thirds of North America.

SPOTTAIL SHINERS are named for a black spot at the base of the tail. They often share the same waters as the emerald shiner, but do not occur as far south.

GOLDEN SHINERS have a deep body with gold coloration and a sharp-edged belly behind the pelvic fins. They may grow to over 1 foot in length. Golden shiners prefer quiet waters, thriving in clear lakes with dense stands of aquatic plants. They are common in southern Canada and the eastern half of the United States.

How to Identify Other Baitfish

In addition to minnows, a wide variety of other fish are used for bait. Small gamefish are popular as bait in some states but are prohibited in others.

MUDMINNOWS, though not true minnows, live in swamps and sluggish streams in many eastern and central states. They have a vertical bar near the rounded tail.

MADTOMS, or *willow cats,* have an adipose fin that continues to the tail. Several species of madtoms are found in quiet rivers and lakes east of the Rockies.

BLUEGILLS have a bluish gill flap with a black lobe. Bluegills and other sunfish, often called *bream,* are widely distributed in North America.

GIZZARD SHAD have a long, last ray on the dorsal fin and a dark spot behind the head. They live in rivers, lakes and reservoirs in the eastern half of the United States.

ALEWIVES have a dark spot behind the head but do not have a long dorsal ray. An ocean fish, they have moved into Atlantic Coast lakes and the Great Lakes.

WHITE SUCKERS have fleshy, coarse lips that protrude from the underside of the head and scales that are larger toward the tail. Young suckers have several blotches on their sides. White suckers are common in lakes and streams throughout much of Canada and the northern two-thirds of the United States.

MOTTLED SCULPINS, known as *bullheads* or *muddlers*, have large pectoral fins. They live in mountain streams of the West, in many eastern states and Canada.

BANDED KILLIFISH have a turned-up mouth and dark bars along the side. They live in lakes and streams of southern Canada and northern and eastern states.

YELLOW PERCH have six to eight dark bars along the side. Widely-introduced, they are most common in lakes in the northern United States and Canada.

CISCOES have a sleek body and an adipose fin (arrow). Also called *lake herring* or *tullibees*, they inhabit large, deep lakes of the northern states and Canada.

RAINBOW SMELT have iridescent, silvery sides; an adipose fin; a pointed snout; a long, narrow body; and large teeth. An ocean species, the fish entered the Great Lakes via the St. Lawrence Seaway. They have also been stocked in many inland lakes in the northern United States and Canada.

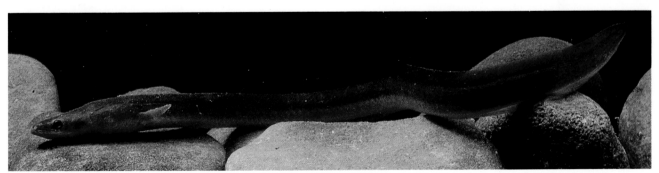

AMERICAN EELS have a fin surrounding the rear half of the body. They reach 4 feet in length. They resemble lampreys, but have jaws rather than round sucking discs. Eels spawn east of the Bahama Islands, but the young migrate to rivers along the Atlantic and Gulf coasts. They swim upstream as far as South Dakota.

Buying Baitfish

Bait shops carry minnows and other baitfish that dealers can easily buy or collect and keep alive. But these species may not always be the best choices for waters in your area. Many of the best types of baitfish can be purchased only in the spring and fall, when cooler weather makes it easier to collect and transport them. As a result, anglers often collect their own baitfish.

If you lack the time or inclination to gather your own baitfish, at least take a few seconds to look at the fish you are buying. When held in captivity, baitfish are under stress and subject to disease. Bait tanks must be periodically disinfected to keep fish healthy. If you buy sick baitfish, chances are they will die before you reach your destination.

Many regions have their own names for common baitfish. For example, in some western states, scul-

pins are called *bullheads*. In the South, fatheads may be sold as *tuffies* or *mudminnows*. Examine your purchase carefully to make sure you are getting the fish you want.

Bait dealers generally keep their baitfish in cold water. When buying baitfish, remember that most of the least hardy and moderately hardy baitfish (page 19) will die if transferred to water more than 10 degrees warmer. *Temper* the fish by allowing their water to warm gradually. Drastic changes in the temperature may not affect the hardier species of baitfish.

Do not buy more baitfish than you can safely transport. If you must carry a large number of minnows over a long distance, place them in a large, aerated cooler or live well, or ask the bait shop operator to oxygen-pack the fish (page 35).

Tips for Buying Baitfish

HEALTHY baitfish form a dense ball in the corner of the bait tank or congregate near bottom. Shiners form looser groups than most other baitfish.

DISEASED baitfish are usually much darker than healthy ones. They school more loosely in a tank and often swim listlessly near the surface.

AVOID buying baitfish with damaged fins, red snouts or fungus growing on the body. Fungus grows as white, cottony patches wherever scales and slime have been rubbed off the fish. Bulging eyeballs and black heads are signs of disease for most kinds of baitfish. Missing scales indicate that baitfish have been handled too much.

Catching Baitfish

The best times to catch baitfish are in early morning or late evening, when they are likely to be in shallow water. Catching them becomes more difficult at midday, when the penetrating rays of the sun drive fish into deeper water. Some species, such as smelt, are caught most easily at night.

Some of the most effective baitfish are not available from bait shops because they are difficult to collect and die quickly if kept in tanks. Fishermen who want to use these species must catch their own by trapping, netting or angling with hook-and-line.

The fisherman who is alert to signs of baitfish activity stands the best chance of catching them. Watch for schools of minnows dimpling the surface, or look for large swirls made by predators chasing schools of baitfish in the shallows. Stand motionless on a low bridge or dock and peer into the water with polarized glasses. You should be able to see any baitfish in the water below.

Trapping

Trapping is an easy way to catch baitfish. Simply bait the trap, set it in the shallows of a lake, stream or pond, and pick it up later. Traps cause less stress and damage to fish than most other collecting devices.

If you trap in a lake with algae covering the surface, be sure to retrieve the trap before dark. The algae produces oxygen during the day but consumes it at night. Baitfish that enter a trap in daylight may die of oxygen starvation if left overnight. Oxygen depletion is seldom a problem in streams or clear lakes.

Most fishermen use commercially-made traps. But to catch madtoms, just string together a dozen beer or soft drink cans and sink them. When removing the madtoms from the cans, avoid touching their sharp pectoral spines because they can inject a poison into the skin that causes a painful reaction.

How to Use a Commercial Trap

SNAP APART the trap and bait it with a few pieces of bread or crackers. If setting the trap in muddy water, attach a marker. In a stream, place a few rocks in the bottom of the trap so the current will not move it.

SET the trap in shallow water. In a river, face it downstream to catch minnows moving upstream. Baitfish funnel into the cone-shaped entrance and cannot escape. Leave the trap several hours or overnight.

Homemade Baitfish Traps

BEER CAN TRAPS for madtoms are made by tying a strong cord to the tabs or cinching it around the can tops. For large madtoms, enlarge the openings slightly. Sink the cans in a marshy river backwater. Madtoms will swim into the openings to find cover. Pick up the cans the next day.

COFFEE CAN TRAPS are made by stapling a 1-inch funnel of window screen around a hole in the plastic lid. Lay the baited trap on its side.

Seining

SEINING is most productive in shallow water. Backwaters, small streams and lake or river shorelines usually hold many baitfish.

A single seine haul can capture enough minnows for a month of fishing. It is the best method for catching baitfish that scatter along lakeshores or in large stream pools.

Most tackle shops sell inexpensive seines. A popular size is 25 feet long and 4 feet deep with ¼-inch mesh. The netting has floats along the top and a heavy lead line or weights across the bottom. The most durable seines are made of nylon or other synthetic material. Unlike cotton, nylon will not rot if stored wet, but it will deteriorate if hung in bright sunlight. Attach two poles, or *brails,* for pulling the seine. Brails can be cut from broom handles or sturdy tree branches.

If possible, land the seine on a gradually tapering shore. To keep fish in the best condition, pull the lead line onto shore, but leave part of the net in the water. Lift the ends so the fish gather in a small pool. Then use a hand net to transfer them into buckets.

How to Pull and Land a Seine

PULL a seine with the outside seiner moving ahead of the person near shore. This keeps many baitfish from swimming around the end of the net.

KEEP the lead line on bottom and the floats on or above the surface. Pulling the net too fast raises the lead line, allowing the fish to escape.

TRAP fish by swinging the outside pole toward shore. Do not lift the net until all of the lead line has been pulled onto shore.

Cast Netting

A cast net enables the solo fisherman to catch bait-fish in open water. Cast nets work best for baitfish that school near the surface. Fish that are near bottom may scatter before the net reaches them. To concentrate fish, many anglers chum with bread, crackers or other foods that float on the surface.

Throwing a cast net is more difficult than most other baitfish collecting techniques, but a little practice will pay off with good catches. When thrown, the net opens into a large cone. Weights fastened around the open end strike the water first, pulling the net down into the water where it surrounds the fish. The angler then pulls a line to close the net and retrieve the baitfish.

Most commercial fishing supply houses and tackle shops carry cast nets. They come in a variety of sizes. A net about 10 feet in diameter is easy to handle and adequate for most situations.

CAST NETS can be thrown as far as 30 feet. They are popular in lakes and reservoirs where schools of baitfish can be spotted near the surface.

How to Throw a Cast Net

TIE the line to your wrist. With the same hand, grasp the net where it is attached to the line. Hold the lead line with the other hand and teeth.

TWIST at the waist and throw the net, spinning it with your arms and shoulders. The net should be open as it strikes the water.

ALLOW the net to sink until it surrounds the baitfish. Quickly pull the retrieving line to draw the net shut; then retrieve it slowly.

Umbrella and Dip Netting

Umbrella and dip nets work best when schools of baitfish are crowded into small areas. Umbrella nets, also called drop nets, are available from commercial fishing supply houses and many tackle shops. They are made of nylon netting 3 to 4 feet square. A metal frame keeps the net spread.

Lower the net with a rope attached to the center of the frame. Pull the net straight up from a dock, pier or anchored boat. If possible, leave the net partially submerged and quickly remove the baitfish with a small hand net.

Many kinds of dip nets are sold at tackle shops. Nylon nets are durable, easy to pull through the water and easy on fish. Those with wire netting are heavy and may scrape off slime and scales. The net should be 1 to 2 feet in diameter and at least 2 feet deep so fish cannot jump out. The handle should be 6 feet or longer. Dip nets work best in shallow rivers and streams, or from docks along lakeshores.

SWEEP the dip net through the water and lift quickly. Many species of baitfish, such as smelt, can be dipped more easily at night.

LOWER an umbrella net. Let it rest on bottom several minutes, then lift quickly. Some anglers throw out corn and other chum to attract baitfish.

Angling With Hook and Line

Angling for baitfish can be productive and enjoyable. Large shiners, chubs and suckers put up a good fight on light tackle. Many fishermen use multiple-hook rigs to catch several alewives or small panfish at a time. Some cast treble hooks into dense schools to snag baitfish.

Use an ultra-light spinning outfit, light-action rod or cane pole to catch baitfish. Small hooks from #12 to #18 are needed for their tiny mouths. The best lures are 1/32- or 1/64-ounce jigs. Fly fishermen use nymphs, dry flies and wet flies ranging in size from #10 to #18. Some anglers use barbless hooks to avoid injuring the fish.

To catch bottom-hugging fish such as suckers and chubs, pinch on a small split-shot and thread a tiny piece of worm or kernel of corn on a #12 or #14 hook. A good technique for many other baitfish is to chum with bread or crackers, then float your bait on the surface.

ANGLING for large golden shiners is a sport in itself. Many fishermen use the big shiners as live bait for trophy largemouth bass (page 44).

HANDLE a baitfish carefully. Try to remove the hook without tearing its mouth. Drop the fish into a container filled with water from the lake or river.

CATCH baitfish on corn, bread balls, pieces of worm, insects, or artificial flies and lures. If you do not have a small lure, tie red thread to a tiny hook.

AERATION adds oxygen to the water, increasing the number of baitfish you can keep alive. Fish require less oxygen in cold water than in warm water, because cold water slows their metabolism. Also, cold water holds more oxygen than warm water. Baitfish rarely die from lack of oxygen in water below 50°F.

Keeping Baitfish

Experienced fishermen know the value of keeping baitfish fresh and healthy. Most gamefish will strike a struggling minnow, but ignore a dead minnow or one that is barely moving.

Baitfish should be kept in oxygenated water at temperatures from 50° to 65°F. To keep them in the best possible condition, a few extra precautions are necessary. It is best to use water from a lake, stream or well. If you must use tap water, add dechlorinating tablets or drops, or let the water stand overnight so the chlorine will evaporate. If you want to keep baitfish longer than a few days, change the water to prevent a build-up of waste products.

The only baitfish species that does not have to be kept in water is the American eel. Eels are amazingly hardy. On their long upriver migrations, many crawl overland to get around dams and other obstructions. If refrigerated in a bed of damp moss, eels will stay alive for up to two weeks.

When ice fishing, the frigid water in a bucket keeps baitfish alive all day. But keeping them between fishing trips is another matter. One solution is to cut a hole in the ice large enough for a perforated bucket. Attach a rope, then sink the bucket below the ice. Bury the rope in slush on the ice. When you return, chop open the hole and lift out the bucket.

BAITFISH CONTAINERS (left to right): Plastic trolling bucket that pulls through the water easily, styrofoam container that allows oxygen to seep in, aerated bucket for keeping baitfish alive in a boat or car, styrofoam container with metal shell for added strength, metal bucket with perforated liner for use in or out of water.

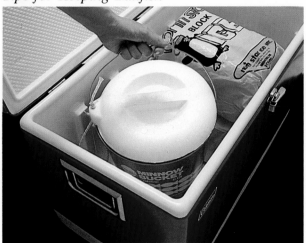

COOLERS with ice keep baitfish at lower temperatures. Ice can also be added to water in the bucket. At home, place the fish in a cool area of the basement.

REFRIGERATORS keep baitfish alive for long periods. When kept at temperatures of 40°F or less, baitfish do not have to be fed.

FLOW-THROUGH CONTAINERS keep baitfish lively, but only if the surface water is cool. If the water is too warm, place the bucket in a cooler.

BARRELS keep baitfish for an extended period. Feed them oatmeal or commercial fish food. Avoid overfeeding; they should eat all of their food in a few minutes.

INNER TUBES are used to float small, perforated garbage cans for keeping shad and other sensitive baitfish. Before moving the boat, put the can in a larger container.

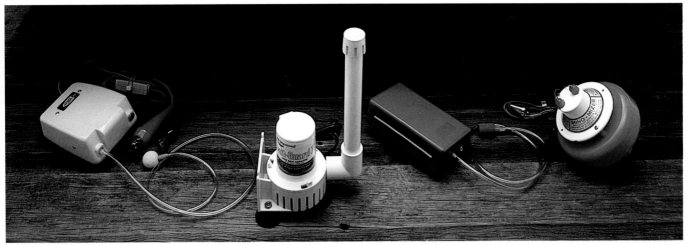

AERATORS operate from flashlight, lantern, and boat batteries, or from other 6- or 12-volt power sources. Converters reduce 12 volts to 6, or 110 volts to 12. Adaptors enable you to plug an aerator into the cigarette lighter of a boat or automobile. Small aquarium aerators plug into 110-volt outlets.

OXYGEN-PACK baitfish for a long trip. Some bait shop operators will put the fish in plastic bags filled with water and pure oxygen. The fish will last several days.

OXYGEN TABLETS produce bubbles when dropped into water. They are useful when driving to your fishing spot or at other times when an aerator is not available.

AVOID overcrowding baitfish. As a general rule, 1 gallon of water will support 1 to 2 dozen small- or medium-size baitfish, or 4 to 8 larger baitfish.

Fishing With Baitfish

Live bait dealers in one midwestern state sell about 2.5 million pounds of baitfish annually. Add to this figure the large number trapped and netted by fishermen, and one begins to realize the enormous popularity of baitfish.

Baitfish cost less than most other baits and can be purchased almost anywhere. They work for a wide variety of fish because all gamefish eat smaller fish at some time in their lives. Large predators such as northern pike and muskies eat fish almost exclusively.

Another reason for the popularity of baitfish is their versatility. When dangled from a bobber, they swim enticingly for hours. They can be trolled or drifted, or cast into weeds and allowed to swim through the tangle. They can be used to tip jigs, spinners and other lures. Fished dead on the bottom or cut into chunks, they will attract scavenging fish.

The natural cycle of baitfish populations has a significant impact on fishing success. In spring, baitfish numbers reach the lowest level of the year. Small fish hatched the previous spring have been subjected to a year of predation by larger fish, birds, insects, crayfish and a host of other predators. Disease has also taken its toll. Those that survived the winter have grown too large for many kinds of gamefish. Because food is scarce, gamefish spend more time cruising the shallows to find baitfish. This explains why shore fishermen often fill their stringers quickly in spring. Good fishing continues as long as natural foods remain scarce.

Most baitfish spawn in spring, but the young fish are too tiny to attract larger fish until a month or two after hatching. By mid-summer, clouds of small baitfish mill about in the shallows, and predators eat their fill in a few minutes.

By fall, predators have once again reduced the baitfish supply, so gamefish must resume their search for food. Fishing continues to improve as fish spend more and more time feeding. But as winter approaches and the water becomes cold, fish eat less and become more difficult to catch.

Lively bait can attract gamefish even when baitfish are plentiful. A gamefish with a full belly may ignore a school of minnows only inches away, but will strike a minnow struggling on a hook.

To improve your chances, inspect the bait often. If it stops swimming actively, replace it. Many anglers stick with a minnow as long as it shows some sign of life. Considering the other expenses involved in a fishing trip, saving a few pennies by conserving baitfish makes little sense.

Anglers use special techniques when fishing is slow. Some fishermen clip a small portion of a baitfish's tail, causing it to swim erratically. In an aquarium, largemouth bass ignored minnows thrown into the water. However, they immediately grabbed a minnow with a clipped tail. Bass facing away from a clipped minnow turned toward the baitfish as soon as it began swimming. The bass probably detected the unusual vibrations with their lateral line sense. Expert jig fishermen sometimes tip a jig with a minnow hooked upside down. The minnow tries to right itself, attracting fish that might otherwise ignore the bait.

Good fishermen select their baitfish carefully. Many seine or trap their own because they are unable to buy a certain size or a species that will remain lively on the hook. Such selectivity may not be necessary when fish are hungry, but it can make a big difference when they are only half-interested in eating.

Crappies & Other Panfish

More crappies are caught on small baitfish than on all other baits and lures combined. Yellow perch, white perch, rock bass, warmouth, white and yellow bass, and some species of sunfish will take minnows.

A variety of baitfish are routinely sold as *crappie minnows*. Fatheads and shiners are the most popular, followed by small dace and chubs. Large crappies, yellow perch and white bass will take a minnow up to 3 inches in length, but in most cases a 1½- to 2-inch minnow works best. Sunfish usually ignore a minnow longer than 1 inch.

When the shallows warm in spring, minnows move into quiet bays and sunny shorelines. The crappies are not far behind. Most shore fishermen use bobbers and minnows, or jig-minnow combinations.

Later in summer, large crappies move out to deeper cover. They frequently hang around mid-lake rock piles, sunken islands or submerged brush. During the day, they may suspend in deep water away from cover. Most fishermen catch them on slip-bobber rigs or tandem hook rigs fished vertically.

When fishing with minnows for other panfish, anglers often use bobber rigs, split-shot rigs or jig-minnow combinations. Some crappie fishermen in the South use welding rod rigs in heavy brush to avoid constant snagging.

How to Make a Welding Rod Rig

DANGLE a minnow on a welding rod rig into brush or timber. Jiggle it to attract crappies. If the rig becomes snagged, drop the welding rod. The downward pull should free the hook. The welding rod also prevents a fish from wrapping the line around branches.

CUT an 8-inch piece of welding rod. Flatten the ends and drill a hole in each. Insert a snap at one end and a snap-swivel at the other. Use a #4 light-wire hook and 20-pound mono. Hook a small minnow through the back. Fish with a shorter rod in dense brush.

How to Fish a Jig and Minnow

HOOK a 1½-inch minnow through the lips on a ¹⁄₁₆- or ⅛-ounce jig tied directly to 4- to 6-pound monofilament. In heavy weeds or brush, use a bobber to suspend the lure and bait just above the cover.

CAST the jig and minnow, letting it sink until it hits bottom. Retrieve slowly, hopping the jig, as shown in this multiple-exposure photograph. Fish usually grab a jig as it drops, so keep a tight line to detect the strike.

How to Rig a Slip-bobber

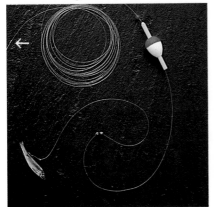

THREAD a commercial slip-knot (arrow), a bead and a slip-bobber on the line. Add split-shot; insert a #4 or #6 hook just below the dorsal fin.

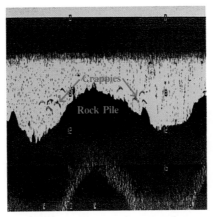

WATCH your graph recorder or flasher to determine the depth of fish. This tape shows crappies suspended off a rock pile in 10 feet of water.

SET the slip-knot for the correct depth by measuring line between your arms. The length of your outstretched arms is roughly equal to your height.

How to Tie and Fish a Tandem Hook Rig

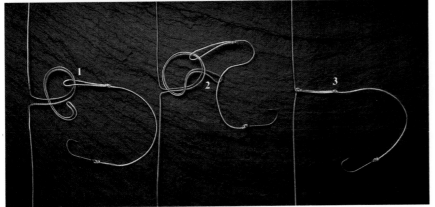

TIE two dropper lines with stiff 20-pound mono and #4 hooks. With 12-pound mono, (1) form a double strand 15 inches from the end; pass it through the dropper loop. (2) Tie an overhand knot, then pass the hook through the doubled line. (3) Snug up knot. Tie on another dropper 15 inches above the first; add a bell sinker to the 12-pound mono. (For illustration, heavy line is used.)

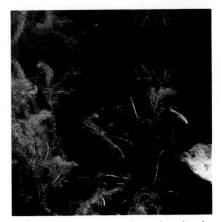

STILL-FISH a tandem hook rig around weeds, brush, stumps or other cover. To find large crappies suspended in open water, troll slowly or drift while varying the depth.

Walleyes

A glint of light off the side of a shiner may be the key to triggering a strike from a stubborn walleye. Emerald shiners are an important food for walleyes in many large lakes. But because emerald shiners are difficult to keep alive, many walleye experts use golden shiners. Other popular baitfish for walleyes include fatheads, common shiners and redtail chubs. Madtoms work well for walleyes in rivers. For average-size walleyes, use 2½- to 3-inch bait-fish. However, a walleye over 5 pounds can easily swallow a 6-inch minnow.

Slow-trolling with a slip-sinker rig probably accounts for more walleyes than any other bait-fishing technique. If you feel even the slightest tug, release the line so the fish can swim off without feeling resistance. Wait until the fish stops, then quickly reel up slack and set the hook.

Baitfish work best in spring and fall. But in northern lakes where natural foods are scarce, baitfish are effective for walleyes year-round. In these waters, dead or preserved baitfish (page 154) work nearly as well as live ones.

How to Tie Slip-sinker Rigs

BASIC SLIP-SINKER RIGS are tied by threading a ¼- to ½-ounce walking sinker on 8- to 10-pound mono. Attach a barrel swivel. Tie 3 feet of 6-pound mono to the swivel, then add a #4 or #6 short-shank hook.

EGG SINKER RIGS are easy to tie. Thread on the sinker, pinch on a small split-shot about 3 feet from the end of the line, and tie on the hook. Avoid rocky bottoms. When snagged, the sinker will slide, fraying the line.

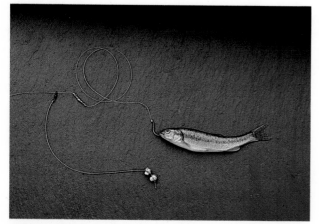

SPLIT-SHOT RIGS include a dropper line with one or two shot. Push the main line through a swivel on the dropper. Tie a barrel swivel to the line; add a leader and hook. When snagged, the shot pulls off, freeing the rig.

SLIDING BOTTOM-WALKER RIGS work well on snaggy bottoms. Attach a snap-swivel to the front eye (arrow) and thread the main line through both swivels. Tie a barrel swivel to the end of the line; add a leader.

Tips for Fishing With a Slip-sinker Rig

TROLL slowly because walleyes rarely strike fast-moving baits. Many anglers backtroll to slow their boats and for better control when following bottom contours. Splash guards on the transom keep out waves.

MARK the spot when you catch a walleye, then work the area thoroughly. Use a commercial marker or make your own from an *H*-shaped piece of styrofoam, a 30-foot string and a lead weight.

SELECT a sensitive rod to detect the subtle bites of walleyes and changes in the type of bottom material. Most experts prefer a graphite, boron, or high-quality fiberglass rod with a fast action.

Other Popular Minnow Rigs

A JIG AND MINNOW works well in spring and fall. Use a plain jig head or a jig that does not hide the minnow. Most anglers prefer yellow or white.

STINGER HOOKS catch short-striking fish. Tie 10-pound mono to the bend of a hook, then pierce the tail with a prong of a #10 treble hook.

FLUORESCENT spinners work well in dark water. Thread on the clevis so the concave side of the blade faces the hook. Add beads and a #4 hook.

Northern Pike & Muskies

A big northern pike or muskie will attack almost anything that swims. Muskrats, ducklings, or a walleye struggling on the end of a fisherman's line are all fair game. But pike and muskies prefer torpedo-shaped fish such as suckers, chubs, shiners, yellow perch, smelt and ciscoes.

If you want to catch a big pike or muskie, select big baitfish. Bait dealers often sell 4- to 5-inch baitfish as *pike minnows.* This size may work for pike under 5 pounds, but a 10-pounder is more apt to take a 7- to

10-inch minnow. Some muskie anglers use 14-inch suckers that exceed 1 pound. With baitfish this size, you must wait several minutes before setting the hook. The fish needs time to mouth the bait, turn it, and swallow it headfirst.

When fishing with large baitfish, many anglers use some type of sliding float. When a conventional sliding float is not available, substitute a clip-bobber. Push in the top button, turn the clip so it rests on the surface of the plastic; then clip it on the line below the slip-bobber knot. When cast, the bobber will slide up the line and stop at the knot.

A lifeless bait holds little appeal for these big predators. When bobber-fishing, hook on a fresh, lively baitfish. Many anglers cast or troll with strip-on spinners to make dead minnows look alive. When fishing in scattered weeds, some anglers cast a spinnerbait or weight-forward spinner (page 71) tipped with a 3- to 5-inch minnow.

Popular Northern Pike and Muskie Rigs

SLOT-BOBBER RIGS are made by first tying a slip-bobber knot (page 70). Place the line in the slot, then turn the end plates. Add a sinker, a steel leader and a baitfish hooked in the upper lip or back with a 2/0 hook.

JIG-MINNOW combinations consist of a ¼- to ½-ounce jig and a 3- to 5-inch baitfish. To prevent fish from biting off the line, attach a 6-inch piece of wire leader material, called a striker. Wrap the ends several times.

How to Rig a Pop-off Bobber

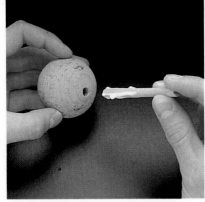

DRILL a hole in a 3-inch cork ball. Cut a 4-inch length of ½-inch dowel and glue it inside the hole. Paint the top of the cork fluorescent orange.

MAKE a ¾-inch slit in the dowel. Tie a 2/0 hook on a 12-inch steel leader and hook a sucker under the dorsal fin. Insert the line into the slit.

A STRIKE jerks the line from the slit, allowing the fish to swim off with no drag. It also gives the angler a straight-line pull for setting the hook.

How to Rig a Strip-on Spinner

INSERT the wire shaft of a strip-on spinner into the mouth of a large sucker, chub or smelt. Push gently until the shaft protrudes from the vent. Use a baitfish long enough to conceal most of the shaft.

ATTACH a double hook by threading it through the loop on the end of the wire shaft. Pull the wire forward to snug up the hook. The tail of the baitfish should be cradled between the hook points.

SET the hook after giving the bass a minute or two to swallow the bait. Keep steady pressure on the fish so it cannot swim back into heavy cover.

Largemouth Bass

A trophy largemouth bass spends most of its day lurking in heavy cover, ignoring the standard lures thrown by fishermen. To catch these big bass, southern anglers hook on foot-long baitfish.

In nature, bass eat yellow perch, bluegills, shad and a wide variety of other fish. Almost any fish will catch bass, but large golden shiners seem to have special appeal.

In early spring, southern fishermen drop 6- to 12-inch shiners into small openings in thick vegetation such as water hyacinth, hydrilla, and milfoil. The shiner swims through the weedy jungle, attracting bass that lurk in the cover. Bass fishermen in other parts of the country use baitfish less often, although fishermen on southern and eastern reservoirs catch many bass on shad. American eels are gaining popularity along the Atlantic Coast.

Yanking bass out of a tangled weedbed requires a stiff rod and 15- to 20-pound line. Most fishermen freeline the shiner. Others attach a bobber to detect strikes and to track the shiner's movement. A weedless hook may be needed in very dense cover.

How to Freeline With Golden Shiners

HOOK a shiner just above the anal fin with a 1/0 to 3/0 hook when fishing shallow. When fishing deep, hook it through both lips and add a sinker. The weight will pull the shiner's nose down, so it swims deeper.

LOB the shiner toward the weeds. It will usually swim into the heavy cover. If it refuses to enter the vegetation, cast it out again. If it still refuses after several tries, replace it with another shiner.

Smallmouth Bass

Smallmouths cruising sun-warmed shallows before spawning feed heavily on minnows. During this time, the flash from a shiner is irresistible.

In summer, when shiners become difficult to keep alive, anglers switch to fathead and bluntnose minnows, chubs, and a variety of other baitfish. Some river fishermen believe that no bait compares to the madtom, or willow cat. Despite their effectiveness, madtoms are not widely used because many bait shops do not carry them.

Unlike largemouths, smallmouth bass prefer small baitfish. Most fishermen favor a 2- to 3-inch minnow, though a slightly larger baitfish may work better for big smallmouths.

Fishermen frequently troll split-shot or slip-sinker rigs over clean sand or gravel bottoms. When fishing the rocky bottoms where smallmouths are found, they turn to bottom-walker rigs which are less apt to snag. Small minnows are also used to tip artificial lures, such as weight-forward spinners (page 71), spin-rigs (page 69), ⅛- to ¼-ounce jigs or straight-shaft spinners.

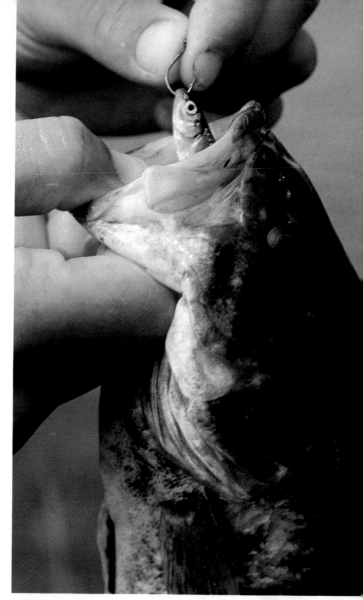

GRAB a smallmouth or largemouth bass by the lower lip when landing it. A firm grip paralyzes the fish, enabling you to remove the hook easily.

Popular Smallmouth Rigs

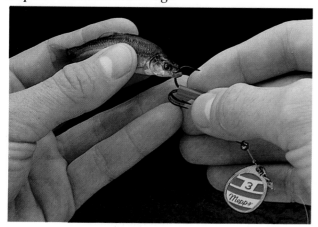

STRAIGHT-SHAFT SPINNERS, such as a #2 or #3 Mepps®, can be tipped with a minnow. Push one prong through both lips. Cast toward a rocky lakeshore or to boulders and eddies in a river. Retrieve slowly.

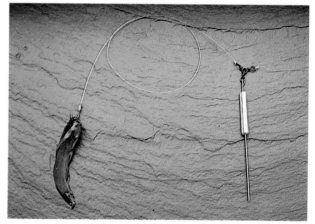

SNAG-PROOF RIGS are tied by attaching an 18- to 24-inch leader to one eye of a Needle Weight™ or other snag-resistant sinker. Add a #4 hook baited with a madtom or shiner. Tie the main line to the other eye.

Catfish

With jaws nearly a foot wide, a big flathead catfish eats fish that most anglers would be happy to catch. Some trotline fishermen use carp and other baitfish weighing up to 2 pounds.

Flatheads prefer live fish. Channel and blue cats also bite on live baitfish, but most are caught on dead fish or fish chunks.

When fishing for large catfish, many anglers use a Wolf River rig to keep the bait fluttering off bottom. For smaller catfish, an egg sinker rig (page 40) or a sliding Wolf River rig (page 73) may work better.

Trotlines and *limblines*, while considered commercial gear in some states, are commonly used on large rivers and reservoirs. A trotline, or *setline*, consists of a dozen or more hooks. A limbline has only a single hook. It is tied to an overhanging branch so the baitfish dangles in the water. Both types of lines are set one day and picked up the next.

How to Use a Wolf River Rig

THREAD a 24-inch leader of 15-pound mono through the eye of a bait needle. Push the line into the mouth and out the vent of a 5- to 7-inch shad. Tie on a 1/0 to 3/0 treble hook.

TIE a three-way swivel to 20-pound monofilament. Attach the baited leader and a 10-inch dropper of 12-pound mono tied to a 3- to 4-ounce pyramid sinker.

CAST into tailwaters where catfish hide among the rocks. This rig works well on rocky bottoms. If the sinker snags, its lighter line will break first so you can salvage the rest of the rig.

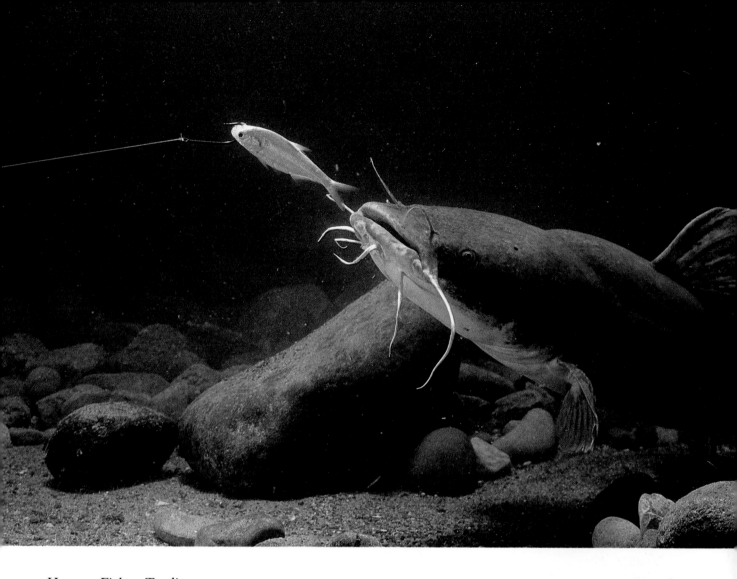

How to Fish a Trotline

TROTLINES have a heavy nylon main line weighted at each end. Lighter dropper lines with 1/0 hooks are spaced every few feet. They are kept in a grooved box to prevent tangling.

SET the trotline at dusk. Lower a weight, then pay out line. Bait each hook with whole or cut shad. Pull the line tight and lower the other weight. Some anglers add floats and markers.

LIFT the trotline the next morning. Do not attempt to hoist a large catfish into the boat because the hook may rip out. Instead, exert steady pressure until the fish tires, then net it.

Striped Bass

In late summer and fall, striped bass slash into schools of shad on the surface of reservoirs. Fishermen pinpoint feeding stripers by watching for gulls diving to pick up injured shad. Then they edge close enough to cast artificial lures. Bass often strike as soon as a lure hits the water.

Fishing for striped bass is not as spectacular the rest of the year, so many anglers switch to bait-fishing and slower, more methodical techniques.

East Coast fishermen use a variety of baitfish for stripers including blueback herring, shad, shiners, eels and alewives. Anglers on the desert reservoirs of the Southwest rely primarily on frozen anchovies. In the south central states from Nebraska to Texas, sunfish, shad, chubs and shiners are popular.

In spring, striper fishermen crowd tailraces on the upper reaches of large reservoirs throughout the country. Others converge on East and West Coast rivers, where spawning stripers have migrated from the ocean. Anglers cast or troll live or cut baitfish, often on slip-sinker rigs. Many shore fishermen cast jigs tipped with baitfish. On eastern rivers, some anglers tip their jigs with 3- to 7-inch American eels, called *pencil eels*.

In summer, stripers in large reservoirs are constantly on the move. Within minutes, a big school may swim from 50 feet of water to within a few feet of the surface. Most anglers troll or drift live baitfish in 20- to 30-foot depths. When trolling in mid-water, many fishermen use bead-chain sinkers so the baitfish cannot twist the line. Slip-sinker rigs are effective when stripers are hugging bottom. On southwestern reservoirs, fishermen troll anchovies on mooching hooks, double needle hooks or large trebles. The anchovies must be kept frozen as long as possible. Once in water, their flesh softens rapidly.

Striped bass do not feed as often during winter, although they continue to wander. They are generally found in deeper water, as far down as 75 feet. To reach these fish, most anglers slow-troll or still-fish with live baitfish.

LARGE STRIPERS are caught on American eels. A favorite saltwater bait on the Atlantic Coast, eels are becoming more popular in fresh water. Some fishermen use eels up to 18 inches long.

How to Rig and Use Sunfish

HOOK a live sunfish through both lips or the back with a 2/0 to 4/0 hook. Attach the ring end of a 1½- to 4-ounce bead-chain sinker to your line and add a 30-inch leader of 12-pound monofilament to the swivel end.

LOCATE striped bass on a graph recorder or depth finder. This graph tape shows a school of striped bass suspended in mid-water. At upper left is a school of threadfin shad (arrow).

Popular Anchovy Rigs

MOOCHING RIGS originated on the West Coast where they are still used to catch salmon. Push the rear hook through the tail and the front hook through one gill and out the other. Adjust the front hook to snug up the line.

DOUBLE NEEDLE HOOKS are rigged by pushing the shaft of a 3/0 or 4/0 hook through the vent and out the mouth. The hooks should point up on each side of the tail. Attach the clip to the hook and tie on the line.

How to Rig and Fish a Jig and Eel

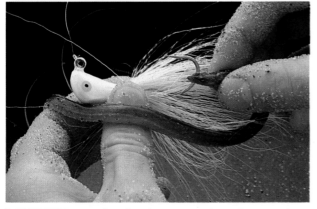

MOISTEN your hands, then press them into sand or sawdust. The grit is essential for holding an eel. Hook it through both jaws with a ½-ounce white or yellow buck-tail. Use a heavier jig for strong current or deep water.

ATTACH a casting bobber about 3 feet above the jig. This rig is effective when stripers are feeding near the surface in tailraces. The weighted float increases casting distance and keeps the bait shallow.

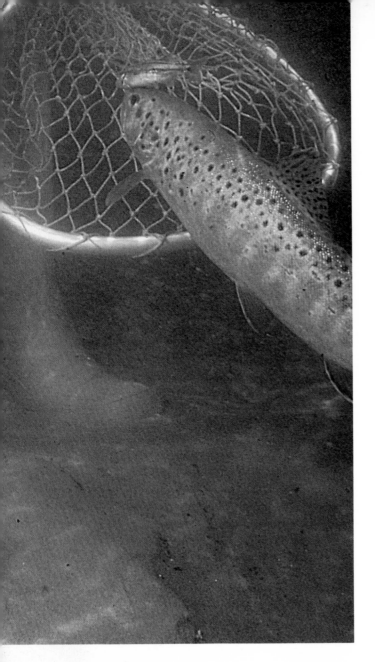

Stream Trout

As trout grow larger, they eat fewer insects and crustaceans, and more fish. All trout eat some minnows, but a big brown relies on fish for most of its diet. If minnows are scarce, a brown trout will not hesitate to eat its own kind.

A fisherman using baitfish stands a better chance of hooking a big brown trout than an angler using other live baits or artificial flies. Stream fishermen catch browns on lip-hooked shiners, dace and fatheads weighted with only a small split-shot. On some midwestern streams, anglers seeking trophy browns still-fish deep pools with 4- to 6-inch sucker fillets. They leave the skin on to keep the fillets on the hook.

Following ice-out, Great Lakes fishermen catch brown trout as large as 25 pounds. Some anglers still-fish or slow-troll with alewives and smelt in shallow bays and near power plant discharges. In summer and fall, browns and rainbows school around Great Lakes piers and tributaries, where they are caught on slip-sinker rigs with alewives.

Sculpins take many trout in western streams. They can be lip-hooked or fished with a double needle hook. Plug-cut herring (page 152) are widely used for huge rainbows in high-altitude lakes of the West.

How to Rig a Sculpin

TIE 6-pound monofilament line to the clip of a #4 or #6 double needle sculpin hook.

PUSH the tapered end of the hook into the fish's vent, through the body and out the mouth.

ATTACH the clip to the hole in the shank to complete the rig. The hook should swing freely on the clip.

Lake Trout

A favorite technique of springtime lake trout anglers is to throw out a dead baitfish, prop the rod on a forked stick, then sit back and wait for a bite. When a laker picks up the bait, it often runs 20 to 30 yards before it stops. A fisherman who forgets to open the bail may suddenly see his rod fly from the stand and disappear into the depths.

Just after ice-out, lakers seek shallower, warmer water. Shore fishermen cast with dead smelt or sucker meat (page 153) on slip-sinker rigs. Because lake trout are scavengers, the bait should be fished on the bottom.

Like most other trout species, lakers shy away from heavy line. Use monofilament no heavier than 10-pound test. Some fishermen switch to 4-pound line when fishing is slow.

Dead baitfish are not used as often in summer because trout are usually scattered and may be suspended off bottom. However, fishermen frequently use sucker meat or meat from other baitfish to tip 1- to 2-ounce bucktail jigs. If you run short of bait, open the stomach of a freshly-caught lake trout. Remove any ciscoes or other baitfish. These soft, partly-digested fish are just as effective as fresh bait.

How to Rig a Smelt

THREAD a ½-ounce egg sinker onto 8-pound mono. Add a barrel swivel and 3 feet of 6-pound leader. Insert a #2 hook through the lips of a 6- to 8-inch smelt.

Salmon

Many a shore fisherman has watched helplessly as a big chinook melts line from his reel and heads for open water. If the angler is lucky, the salmon may stop to swallow the baitfish.

Great Lakes salmon begin congregating near stream mouths weeks before spawning. Starting in late summer, anglers pack breakwaters, piers, docks and shoreline points in hopes of catching a coho or a chinook. Many use some type of floating rig to keep the baitfish off bottom where it sways in the current to attract salmon.

On many New England lakes, fishermen troll sewed baitfish to catch land-locked salmon. Using an eyeless snelled hook, they sew a 10- to 15-pound mono leader into a smelt so the body is slightly curved. When pulled through the water, the smelt wobbles slowly. Too much curve causes the smelt to spin; not enough curve results in little or no action.

West Coast salmon fishermen use plug-cut baitfish extensively. Cutting and rigging methods are shown on page 153.

FLOATING BALL RIGS are made by pegging a Styrofoam® or balsa-wood ball to the line just above the hook, or by attaching a small piece of Styrofoam to the hook shaft. Add an egg sinker, 18-inch leader and #2 hook.

How to Make a Sewing Hook Rig

SEW a baitfish by (1) pushing a snelled hook down through the lower lip and then twice through the head, forming two large loops. (2) Just behind the gill, push the hook into the body and back out. (3) Reinsert the hook in the exit hole and continue the same sewing procedure over the length of the fish. Grab the loop (blue arrow) made when you passed the hook through the head the second time. (4) Pull until the stitches tighten and the fish bends. Grab the other loop (white arrow). (5) Snug up the line.

Ice Fishing

Baitfish offer many advantages to ice fishermen. A minnow weighted with a small split-shot will swim around in a large circle. Other baits cover less territory so they do not attract as many fish.

Baitfish are extremely hardy in winter. A hooked minnow may live only a few minutes in warm water, but will swim tirelessly for hours when fished through the ice. Frigid water slows the action of most other baits.

Nearly all bait shops carry some type of baitfish in winter. But many types of insects, crustaceans and amphibians are difficult if not impossible to find. Ice fishermen use live baitfish almost exclusively for crappies, yellow perch, walleyes, northern pike and pickerel. Most anglers prefer a minnow on a plain hook. Jigs and ice flies tipped with tiny minnows also work well. Lake trout fishermen still-fish on bottom with dead smelt or ciscoes.

Anglers generally prefer smaller minnows in winter than in summer. However, a big pike will swallow an 8- to 10-inch baitfish regardless of the season.

SWEDISH PIMPLE®-MINNOW RIGS are effective for many fish including walleyes, yellow perch and crappies. Lift the lure slowly, then let it flutter down until it settles. Fish usually strike just before the lure stops moving.

How to Use a Tip-up

TIP-UPS have a wooden frame, a flexible steel spring with a small flag on the end, and a reel that operates under water so it will not freeze up. When a fish grabs the bait, a trip mechanism releases the bent spring which pops up to display the flag.

NORTHERN PIKE grab the bait, then swim off slowly. Look into the hole to see the underwater reel. When it stops turning, lift the tip-up, grab the line and jerk hard to set the hook. Play the fish until it tires, then pull it from the hole.

Worms & Leeches

Worms

The earthworm is the most widely-used bait in North America and is one of the easiest natural baits to collect and keep.

Hundreds of earthworm species are found throughout the continent. All have the same general shape but vary widely in size and color. Although most species prefer rich, loamy soil, a few kinds live in sand, clay and even acid soils.

An earthworm literally eats its way through the soil, usually consuming its own weight in organic material every 24 hours. As it crawls, it leaves *castings* of humus-like material that enrich the soil.

Worms do not have eyes or ears, but rely on sensory cells that are extremely sensitive to light. This explains why fishermen rarely find earthworms above ground during the day.

Many worms, such as the nightcrawler, feed on the surface after dark, especially on damp, calm nights. The nightcrawler often anchors its tail inside the burrow, then extends its body to search for food. If disturbed, it quickly withdraws into the burrow.

Some types of earthworms are sensitive to vibrations in the ground. In southern states, collectors draw grunt worms to the surface by a unique method called *fiddling* or *grunting* (page 59). Hundreds of worms may be picked up during a single fiddling operation.

Each earthworm has male and female organs but is unable to fertilize its own eggs. Worms mate by lying side by side and fertilizing each other's eggs. The thick, dark collar on earthworms produces a cocoon, or sac, which contains the developing eggs. Tiny worms emerge two to three weeks after the adult deposits its cocoon in moist soil.

Worms have the ability to regenerate a lost tail or head. Some species can form two complete worms after being cut in half.

In North America, fishermen collect and use several types of worms known by a variety of descriptive common names. Some are commercially raised. The worms most commonly used for bait include:

NIGHTCRAWLER. Sometimes called the *dew* or *rain worm,* the native nightcrawler appears on roads and sidewalks after spring rains. Average length is 6 to 7 inches, but some are 10 inches or longer. Its color varies from brownish-pink to purplish-red.

GARDEN WORM. Often called the *angleworm* or *fishworm,* the garden worm is usually pinkish-red, but varies from gray to yellow and even to pale blue. It averages 3 to 4 inches in length.

LEAF WORM. The leaf worm resembles a small nightcrawler. Seldom exceeding 4 inches in length, it has a tail that is somewhat flattened.

GRUNT WORM. The grunt worm is the general name for several kinds of worms that are collected by fiddling. They average 6 inches in length. Color varies from pink to gray or brown.

MANURE WORM. The manure worm is red with whitish bands along its 3- to 4-inch body. It is raised by bait suppliers in the South and sold as the *red worm.* Another commercially-grown type is the *red wiggler,* which grows to about 2 inches in length.

GRAY NIGHTCRAWLER. Commercial worm growers raise gray nightcrawlers in a mixture of white sand and peat. The worms are a pinkish-gray color with a collar that may be brown or pink. A fast-growing type, the gray nightcrawler averages 4 inches in length. It is difficult to hold because it thrashes violently when touched.

AFRICAN NIGHTCRAWLER. Raised commercially, the African nightcrawler can withstand warmer temperatures than other worms. An active type, it will crawl out of uncovered bait boxes. It is 3 to 4 inches long and similar in color to the native nightcrawler.

Top to bottom: Nightcrawler, Garden Worm, Leaf Worm, Grunt Worm, Manure Worm, Red Wiggler, Gray Nightcrawler, African Nightcrawler.

Collecting Worms

The earthworms used by fishermen can normally be found within a foot or two of the surface or above ground in decaying organic matter. In winter or during hot, dry weather, worms may burrow as deep as 15 feet.

Nightcrawlers and other worms breathe through their skin. When heavy rains flood their tunnels, crawlers move to the surface, often leaving their burrows entirely. Then they are easy to collect. But when their tails are anchored in the burrows, crawlers are difficult to catch because they quickly withdraw back into their holes.

Cool, calm, rainy evenings in spring and fall are the best times to gather nightcrawlers. To locate likely areas, drive around at night during a rain. Watch the road for crawlers and other worms. Another clue is a flock of robins in the same yard day after day.

Lawns, golf courses, parks and baseball fields are good places to collect crawlers. But not all grassy

Tips for Collecting Nightcrawlers

GRAB a nightcrawler firmly by the head. The worm has several rows of tiny bristles which enable it to grip the walls of its burrow (cross section). Exert steady pressure until the worm tires and loosens its grip.

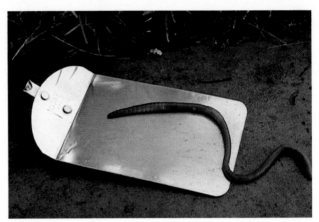

GATHER nightcrawlers and other worms after a heavy rain. Use a metal spatula to scoop them from streets, driveways and sidewalks.

COVER your flashlight lens with a white plastic bag or red cellophane to avoid spooking crawlers. Wear tennis shoes and step lightly, because excessive vibrations will scare them back into their holes.

areas have worms. Some golf courses are chemically treated to control nightcrawlers and other worms.

To check for nightcrawlers, walk across the grass of a lawn or golf course. Soil with a healthy population of crawlers will feel bumpy underfoot. The bumps are the hardened castings of the worms.

Many fishermen search for nightcrawlers, garden worms and leaf worms in compost piles. To make a compost pile, dump grass clippings, leaves, coffee grounds and other organic material over rich, black dirt. It may take a year for the materials to decay enough to attract worms.

Tips for Collecting Other Worms

Most anglers dig in moist, rich soils to find garden worms. In rural areas, check freshly-turned clumps of soil in plowed fields during spring and fall. Leaf worms are most often found under piles of rotting leaves or in decaying logs or stumps.

In southeastern states, anglers gather grunt worms in pine-studded woodlands with acid soil. Hillsides are good spots when conditions are wet; lowlands are best during dry periods.

Manure worms can be collected around stables, barnyards and other places that have manure or decaying organic matter.

TURN OVER boards and rocks to find garden and leaf worms when the soil is damp. Trout fishermen collect worms by rolling over logs along streams.

FIDDLING, or grunting, is a technique used in the South for collecting grunt worms. Rub an axe or piece of steel across the top of a board driven into the ground. The vibrations draw grunt worms to the surface.

SPRINKLE your garden or flower bed for several hours late in the afternoon, then dig with a garden fork early the next morning. If the soil is dry, it may take a full day of soaking to bring worms up from deep in the ground.

Keeping, Raising and Conditioning Worms

If you do a lot of fishing, it pays to have an old refrigerator for storing worms and other live bait. Garden worms and nightcrawlers will stay healthy for months if kept at temperatures between 40° and 60°F. You can also keep worms in a root cellar or in the coolest area of your basement.

Earthworms are stored in a variety of commercial and homemade containers. The type of bedding is more important than the type of worm box. For long-term storage, commercial beddings are ideal. Most consist of finely-ground newspaper mixed with soil, but some are made of sphagnum moss combined with other plant fibers. Worms can also be kept in moist shredded paper.

To store worms, spread a 4-inch layer of bedding in your worm box. As a general rule, 1 square foot of commercial bedding is adequate for about 50 night-crawlers or 150 smaller worms. Lay the worms on the bedding. After several hours, remove any worms that have not tunneled in. Over the next several weeks, check the bedding every three or four days for dead or dying worms.

If kept cool in commercial bedding, worms do not have to be fed for at least three months. However, they will shrink and lose some of their vitality. To keep worms fat and healthy, add small amounts of commercial worm food. Be careful not to overfeed them. If there is more food than the worms can eat, it will rot, increasing the chance of disease. Crawlers can also be fattened by *conditioning,* described on the opposite page.

Some anglers raise red worms in pits filled with a mixture of three parts soil and one part decomposed leaves and other plant material. Where the soil is hard clay or rock, they use a galvanized metal tub in a shady spot above ground or in a cool basement.

Feed the worms a commercial food or your own mixture of vegetable shortening and cornmeal at a ratio of one part to two parts (by weight). Crumble the food and mix it into the top 2 inches of soil. Examine the soil periodically to see if the worms have eaten the food. Feed them no more than they will eat. Sprinkle water over the pit every two weeks to keep the soil slightly damp throughout.

You can begin harvesting the worms within 60 to 90 days. Newly-hatched worms reach full size in 6 months. Three cubic feet of soil should produce 3000 to 5000 red worms per year.

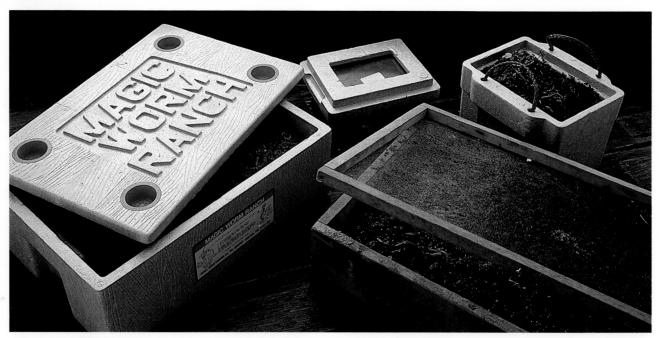

WORM CONTAINERS are made of fiberboard, styro-foam or other porous materials that allow oxygen to penetrate but keep out water. They should have tight-fitting lids to keep the bedding moist and to prevent the worms from crawling out. Some fishermen make their own worm boxes of wood and window screen. Containers used on fishing trips should be well insulated. Some have refreezable ice packs built into the cover.

How to Make a Worm Pit

BUILD a 3 × 4-foot box of wood and screen for breeding and raising red worms. Place the box in a 3-foot deep pit. The site should be in heavy shade and have well-drained soil.

FILL the worm box with layers of rich soil and decayed leaves. Scatter about 200 worms over the bed, then return in several hours to remove any that did not burrow into the soil.

COVER the box to protect the worms from heavy rains and hot sun, and to keep them from crawling out. Replace the soil once a year. Remove worms as needed.

How to Condition Nightcrawlers

SELECT a dozen large nightcrawlers one or two days before a fishing trip. Rinse the worms and place them in a plastic carton half-filled with cool, damp worm bedding.

ADD strips of wet paper to the carton and crawlers (cross section). Mound the paper above the carton and press the lid into place to create a pressure pack. Place the carton in a refrigerator or cooler for 24 to 36 hours.

CONDITIONING makes crawlers larger and more vigorous. The crawler at right was the same size as the other worm. During conditioning, it absorbed water from the paper, swelling to nearly twice normal size.

Leeches

Leeches inhabit lakes, ponds, marshes and slow-moving streams throughout most of North America. All leeches have sucking disks at both ends. The mouth is located in the smaller disk at the head end. Leeches use the large disk on the tail only for clinging to objects.

Most leeches eat dead animals. Some species such as the horse leech digest the skin of live animals and feed on the tissue. A few kinds, such as the medicine leech, are called *bloodsuckers*. They have jaws which actually cut through skin to reach blood vessels and tissue.

Fish eat many types of leeches, but only the ribbon leech is widely used as bait. A few anglers have found tiger leeches to be good panfish bait. Medicine and horse leeches are not as effective.

SEPARATE ribbon and tiger leeches from horse leeches by placing them in a steep-sided bucket. Horse leeches have a more powerful sucking disk, which they use to climb the sides of the bucket.

RIBBON LEECHES squirm actively when held. A ribbon leech has a firmer body than a horse leech and body striations or grooves that are less pronounced.

COLOR of ribbon leeches varies from pure black to light brown. Some have a brown or olive background with many black spots.

TIGER LEECHES are smaller and slimmer than ribbon leeches. They twist and turn violently in the hand. The tiger leech has two to four rows of faint black spots extending down the back.

AVOID medicine leeches and horse leeches. These soft-bodied types are limp and lifeless in the hand and on the hook. The medicine leech (top) has a reddish-orange belly and rows of red dots down the back.

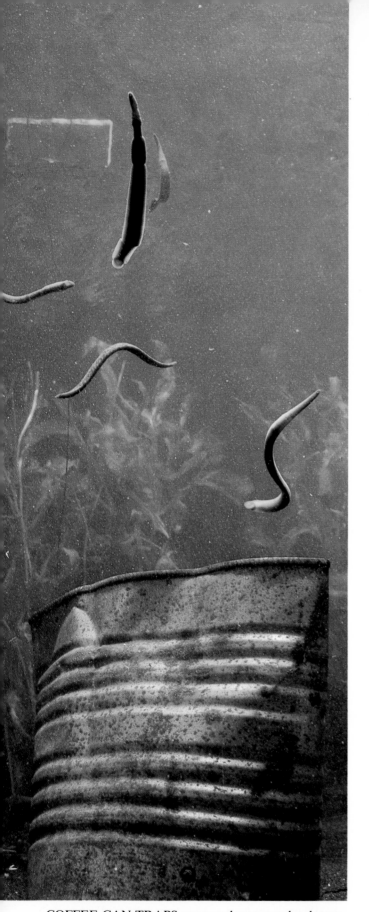

Catching and Keeping Leeches

Leeches are available from bait dealers throughout the north central states, but are rarely sold in other parts of the country. Fortunately, trapping leeches is not difficult. Use coffee cans or gunnysacks baited with fish heads or fresh beef kidneys, liver or bones. Boards smeared with fish oil also work.

During winter, when leeches become dormant, trapping them is nearly impossible. But when ponds

PONDS rimmed with cattails or other shoreline vegetation are ideal for leeches. Those with heavy blooms of algae produce more leeches than clear waters. Leeches feed on microscopic animals that eat the algae.

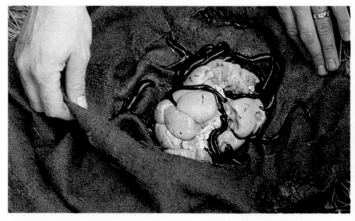

COFFEE CAN TRAPS are popular among leech trappers. Place bait in the can, then crimp the top. Leeches are sensitive to light and will quickly abandon a trap if sunlight penetrates the can.

GUNNYSACKS attached to ropes and tossed into shallow water are effective leech traps. Bait with fresh beef kidneys or liver. Leeches will squeeze through the fabric to reach the bait.

warm to 50°F in spring, they begin searching for food and will swim into traps. By mid-summer, their numbers decline as the adults deposit cocoons and die. The young leeches begin to appear in fall.

Ponds with lush growths of cattails, lily pads and algae support the largest numbers of leeches. Good leech ponds often have healthy populations of fathead minnows. Shortly after spawning in summer, many fatheads die off, providing an abundant supply of food for leeches. However, the presence of gamefish means that bait leeches are not common.

Leeches are easy to keep alive. They are not as sensitive to temperature changes as minnows, and they require relatively little oxygen. But they will soon die if left on a boat seat in the hot sun.

If trapped in spring, leeches can be kept alive until fall. Even without food, they shrink only slightly and remain in good condition.

SET traps late in the day. Place them where the wind creates water currents that carry the smell of the bait. Traps set in these areas will attract more leeches than traps in sheltered places.

PICK UP traps early in the morning, before sunrise if possible. Add straw and rocks to the traps if you are unable to lift them early. Leeches will crawl into crevices in the rocks and straw to escape sunlight.

REFRIGERATE leeches for long-term storage. Styrofoam coolers or minnow buckets are best for storing large quantities. Keep small amounts in plastic containers. When fishing, bring only enough leeches for the trip.

CHECK leeches every three or four days. Pour them into a strainer and discard any that are dead or appear sluggish. Rinse the leeches and return them to a container with cool, dechlorinated water.

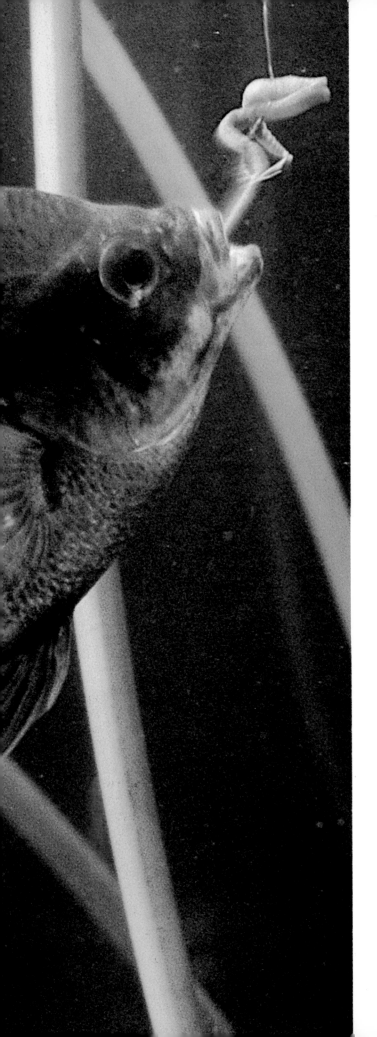

Fishing With Worms & Leeches

Fishermen who use worms and leeches consider them interchangeable as bait. Anglers often carry both, then experiment to see which works the best. Leeches should not be used in water colder than 50°F because they ball up on the hook, refusing to uncoil and swim.

The worms and leeches used for bait are seldom part of the natural diet of gamefish. Heavy rains wash some earthworms into streams and lakes; otherwise, fish rarely see them. Ribbon and tiger leeches are scarce in fishing waters because fish quickly devour them.

Worms appeal to nearly every type of gamefish. Anglers using worms for bait can never be certain what they will catch next. Although nearly any kind of worm will attract fish, anglers usually select worms according to size. Some fishermen believe that a colorful red wiggler will catch more fish than a drab garden worm.

Leeches are becoming popular throughout many northern states but are seldom used in the South. In some areas, leeches have taken so many walleyes that fishermen and resort owners have tried to have them banned as bait.

Not all kinds of leeches attract fish. The leech species that live in waters with gamefish populations usually make poor bait. Most gamefish ignore horse leeches. Either the scent of the horse leech repels fish or it lacks the action of bait leeches.

Although dead worms or leeches may work for bullheads and sunfish, fresh, lively bait will increase your chances of catching most fish. Nibbling panfish will quickly kill a worm or leech. Check your bait often to make sure it is fresh. When a worm turns soft and does not react when touched, replace it. Change a leech when it loses its flattened shape.

Sunfish & Other Panfish

Generations of fishermen have proved that earthworms are an excellent bait for most panfish, especially sunfish, yellow perch and rock bass. Insects and crustaceans will sometimes catch more fish, but worms are generally more reliable.

The smaller varieties of worms work best. Most panfish have small mouths and will only nibble at a worm that is too big. If using a nightcrawler, an inch-long piece is usually sufficient. Some anglers gob a large ball of worms on the hook, making it nearly impossible for panfish to swallow the bait.

Many fishermen have discovered that 1- to 2-inch ribbon leeches sometimes outfish worms. Rather than throw away leeches that are too small for walleyes or smallmouth bass, save them for panfish. Tiger leeches, though not widely available at bait shops, have good potential as a panfish bait. They have an intense action, and fishermen who have tried them have found they work just as well as ribbon leeches.

How to Fish a Bobber Rig

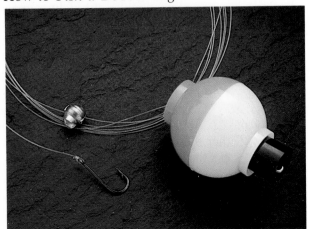

TIE a #8 or #10 hook on 2- to 6-pound monofilament line. Attach a small bobber. Pinch on enough split-shot for balance about 8 inches above the hook.

HOOK small worms several times but let the ends dangle. Thread on a piece of nightcrawler, leaving one end free. Hook small leeches through the neck or sucker.

Popular Lure-Worm Combinations

SPINNER-WORM combinations work well for yellow perch and rock bass. Add enough split-shot 12 inches above the hook to sink the bait to the desired depth.

JIGS AND WET FLIES can be tipped with small pieces of worm. White, yellow and fluorescent green and orange lures are the most popular.

SPIN-RIGS are baited with a worm or leech. Cast, then let the lure *helicopter* to bottom (multiple exposure). Retrieve in sharp jerks, pausing to let the lure sink.

CAST the bait into pockets in lily pads or other weeds. Adjust the bobber so the bait dangles 6 to 12 inches off bottom. If nothing bites, cast to another pocket.

LOWER a leech or worm onto a spawning bed. With a cane pole and small float, you can place the bait directly over the bed without spooking the fish.

Walleyes

In summer, when walleyes are sluggish and well-fed on small baitfish, most anglers switch from minnows to leeches and nightcrawlers. The wiggling action of a crawler or the rippling motion of a leech may entice a walleye to bite.

During hot weather, walleyes frequently suspend several feet off bottom. To keep the bait at the level of suspended fish, dangle a worm or leech from a slip-bobber. Leeches work better than worms because they writhe constantly, even when the bobber is motionless. When drifting or trolling, anglers catch suspended walleyes on slip-sinker rigs and floating jigs tipped with a crawler or leech. Or they inflate a crawler so it glides a few feet above bottom.

When walleyes are not suspended, use a slip-sinker rig and keep the bait near bottom. A walleye inhales a leech or nightcrawler with one quick gulp. Wait a short time to make sure the fish has swallowed the bait, then set the hook. If bobber-fishing, do not wait as long because the fish may detect resistance from the float and drop the bait.

Walleyes prefer baits that move naturally. When trolling or casting, hook a crawler through the tip of the head or a leech through the sucker. If nibbling panfish are a problem, hook the leech through the leathery neck to keep it on the hook.

Rigs and Techniques for Suspended Walleyes

FLOATING RIGS for walleyes include (1-4) jig heads made of hard foam, (5) foam bead that can be adjusted to any position on the line, (6) soft, air-filled jig head with a stinger hook.

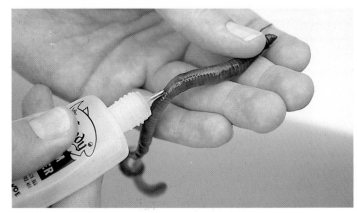

WORM BLOWERS are used to inflate nightcrawlers. Squeeze a bubble of air into the head portion. Adding air to the tail section makes the nightcrawler float vertically so it appears unnatural.

How to Use a Slip-bobber

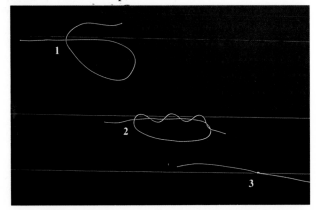

TIE a slip-bobber knot by (1) making a loop from an 8-inch piece of dacron or nylon line. (2) Push one end through the loop and wrap it around the fishing line three times. (3) Snug up the knot and clip the ends.

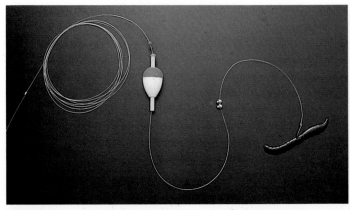

THREAD on a small bead, then the slip-bobber. Pinch on enough split-shot to balance the bobber and tie on a #6 or #8 short-shank hook. Hook a ribbon leech through the sucker or the middle of the body.

PLUGS baited with crawlers may be more effective than unbaited lures, although crawlers interfere with the action of some plugs. For walleyes just off bottom, let out line until the lure ticks bottom, then reel up several turns.

WEIGHT-FORWARD SPINNERS tipped with crawlers work well for suspended fish. Use the countdown system. Cast, then count while the lure sinks. Begin your retrieve at different counts to find the depth of fish.

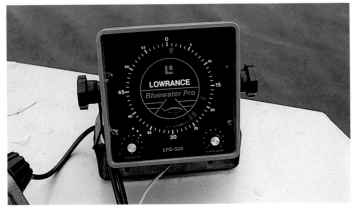

WATCH for suspended fish on your depth finder. Adjust the slip-bobber knot so the bait will hang at the level of the fish. If you do not have a depth finder, keep moving the knot until you find walleyes.

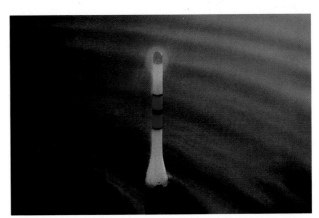

LIGHTED SLIP-BOBBERS, powered by tiny lithium batteries, are handy for night fishing. In spring and fall, anchor around shallow reefs and shoals where walleyes feed after dark.

Bullheads & Catfish

All a bullhead fisherman needs to fill a stringer is a tin can full of worms. Earthworms are also effective for catfish, especially channels and blues, although many diehard catfishermen prefer stinkbaits, blood baits or large baitfish.

Bullhead fishermen generally use two or three small worms on a long-shank hook. The long hook provides additional leverage for removing the barb from a bullhead's mouth. Because bullheads have poor eyesight, the exposed shank does not keep them from biting. Most anglers attach a small fixed-sinker and fish the worms on bottom. Some add a bobber and dangle the bait just off bottom.

Most catfishermen use one or two large crawlers on single or treble hooks that can be hidden by the bait. Others gob as many as six nightcrawlers on a long-shank hook, piercing each worm at least twice. River fishermen sometimes use a sliding Wolf River rig to keep the bait from drifting with the current. With this rig, a catfish can pick up the bait and run without feeling resistance.

In the South, jug-fishing for catfish is popular on reservoirs and slow-moving rivers. Fishermen suspend nightcrawlers, shad, chicken livers or other baits from bleach jugs or 2-liter plastic soft drink bottles. Paint the bottoms fluorescent orange to signal a strike.

How to Tie a Bullhead Rig

ATTACH a #6 or #8 long-shank hook to 6-pound mono-filament line. Hook on two or three worms and add a rubber-core sinker 10 to 12 inches above the bait. A bobber is optional.

How to Jug-fish

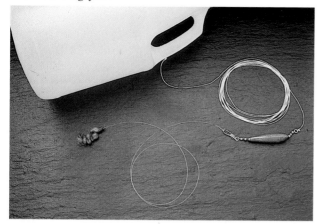

TIE a 5- to 15-foot length of braided dacron line to a jug or 2-liter soft drink bottle. A 20- to 30-pound mono leader and a sinker are optional. Tie on a 1/0 to 3/0 hook baited with a single nightcrawler or gob of crawlers.

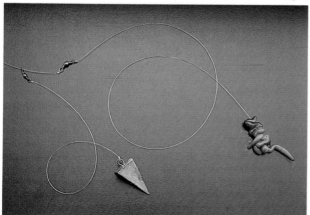

SET the jugs or bottles in a slow-moving stretch of river or in slack water areas of tailraces. A bobbing jug or tipped-up bottle means a catfish has grabbed the bait.

How to Tie and Use a Sliding Wolf River Rig

SLIDE a 20-pound dropper line with a 4-ounce pyramid sinker onto 30-pound line. Tie on a swivel, then add 2 feet of 20-pound monofilament leader with a 1/0 hook gobbed with crawlers.

RETRIEVE the float quickly after it starts to bob or when the orange bottom tips upright. Lift small catfish into the boat. Play a large catfish until it tires, then net it.

CAST the rig with a level-wind reel and a stout, 12-foot cane pole to handle the heavy weight and to increase casting distance. Prop the pole on shore and make sure the fish can take line freely.

Trout

When heavy rains or melting snow cause streams to run high and muddy, most anglers stay home. But experienced fishermen dig up some worms and head for the nearest trout stream. They know that trout feed heavily when rising water dislodges food from the stream bottom and washes in worms and insects. Worms can still be effective when streams clear up, but the fisherman must present the bait more carefully to avoid spooking the trout.

Small worms work best for most trout, although a large trout may prefer a whole nightcrawler. Trout fishermen rarely use leeches, but those who have tried them report excellent results.

Most stream fishermen cast a worm upstream, then let it drift downstream (page 100). Other anglers prefer the downstream drifting technique.

In lakes, fishermen locate the proper temperature zone, then bobber-fish or troll with a worm or leech in that band of water. Some anglers inflate a crawler (page 70) so the worm floats off bottom where it is more visible to trout.

How to Drift a Worm Downstream

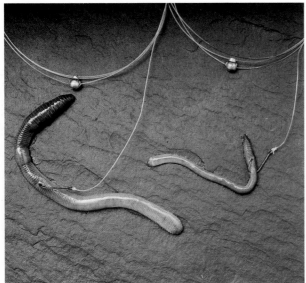

HOOK a nightcrawler through the middle with a #8 hook, then add a small split-shot. If using a smaller worm, push a #10 hook through the collar.

DRIFT the worm downstream by paying out line to keep pace with the current. The bait should drift at the same speed as the current so it appears natural to trout.

THERMOMETERS determine the probable depth of trout. Browns and rainbows prefer water about 60°F, while most other trout species seek water from 50° to 55°F. Use a Deptherm® or electric thermometer for sub-surface readings.

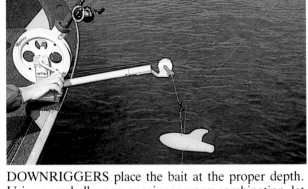

DOWNRIGGERS place the bait at the proper depth. Using a cowbell-worm or spinner-worm combination, let out 50 to 100 feet of line, then attach the line to a release mechanism on the cable. Lower the *bomb* to the desired depth and begin trolling.

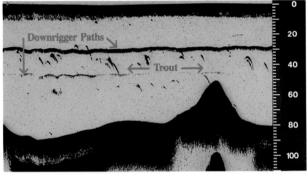

GRAPH RECORDERS pinpoint the location of suspended fish. This graph tape shows a layer of brown trout suspended between 30 and 40 feet. The black lines are the downrigger paths. Troll with the downrigger bombs just above the fish.

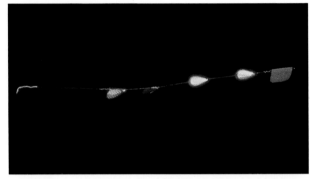

COWBELLS tipped with worms work well for trout in lakes. Flash from the large spinner blades draws trout close enough to see the worm trailing behind. For best results, troll cowbells slowly. At fast speeds, the action is too violent.

AVOID slack line. It may cause the split-shot or hook to snag on bottom. The current will form a large bow in the line, making it difficult to detect a bite.

AVOID tight line because it pulls the worm off bottom, preventing it from moving with the current. The worm will appear unnatural, so trout are likely to ignore it.

Smallmouth Bass

A catfish or bullhead fisherman is sometimes surprised by a big smallmouth bass that suddenly rockets from the water and speeds downstream with his worm. Although most anglers do not consider worms a top smallmouth bait, experts know that a smallmouth will seldom refuse a nightcrawler.

Smallmouth fishermen often use nightcrawlers with slip-sinker rigs. To keep the crawler out of rocks, use a floating jig head or some other type of floating rig (page 70). You can also tip a jig or spinner with a worm or small piece of nightcrawler.

Many anglers are convinced that ribbon leeches work even better than crawlers. When guides in the north central states first discovered leeches, they recorded spectacular smallmouth catches from lakes which many people thought were fished out. Leeches can also be fished on slip-sinker rigs or hooked on artificial lures. Many fishermen use slip-bobbers to suspend leeches over rocky bottoms. Another popular technique is freelining. Simply cast an unweighted leech toward shoreline cover and let it swim about on its own.

Tips for Fishing Smallmouth Bass

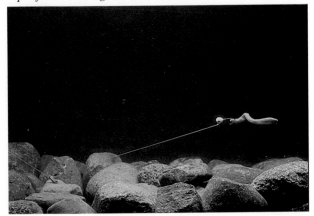

TIE ON a floating jig to prevent the leech or crawler from constantly snagging in rocks. A ⅛- or ¼-ounce slip-sinker keeps the bait close to bottom.

FREELINE a leech near a rocky shore. Reel slowly, pausing to let the leech swim. To cast an unweighted leech, use ultra-light spinning gear and 4-pound mono line.

Largemouth Bass

After a cold front, when largemouth bass bury themselves in the weeds and refuse to bite, a lively worm or leech may be the perfect bait. Rig a night-crawler Texas-style or on a slip-sinker rig similar to those used for walleyes (page 40). Work the worm along bottom near weedlines and other areas with dense cover. If fish seem to be biting short, use a worm harness (page 79).

A jumbo ribbon leech can also be fished from a slip-sinker rig but may be more effective if dangled from a sliding float. A big bass that refuses a trolled bait may strike a leech squirming beneath a float.

Jiggerpoling is an unusual technique for fishing big bass. Fishermen tie a short length of heavy line to a cane pole, then add a treble hook gobbed with worms. To attract bass, they slap the rod tip on the surface. Jiggerpoling is usually done in shallow water choked with timber, weeds or other cover. To insure against losing a large fish, some anglers tie the line to the butt end of the pole, then wind the line around the rod tip. If the tip breaks, the angler can fight the bass with the butt.

How to Rig a Nightcrawler Texas-style

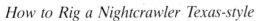

SLIP a small cone sinker onto your line and tie on a 1/0 plastic-worm hook. Insert the point about ½ inch into the head of the worm.

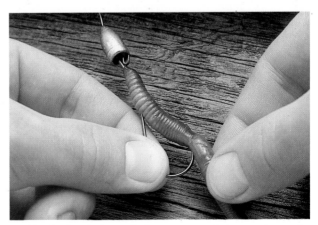

PUSH the hook through the worm until the eye is nearly covered by the worm's head. Rotate the hook a half turn, then bury the point.

Short-striking Fish

One of the most frustrating problems in fishing is continually losing your bait to short-striking fish. Earthworms present a greater problem than other baits because their bodies tear so easily.

Panfish tend to bite short more often than larger fish. But there are times, especially after cold fronts and thunderstorms, when walleyes, bass and trout seem impossible to hook. These fish are not feeding actively, but only nipping at the worm.

One solution is a harness with a hook near the worm's tail. But a harness often reduces the number of bites, because the line dangling along the side makes the worm appear unnatural. To solve this problem, some fishermen use a threaded worm harness with a treble hook at the end of the worm, so they can set the hook immediately.

Another option is to give the fish more time to swallow the bait. With this technique, you run the risk of the fish spitting out the hook. If this happens, switch to a smaller hook and lighter line. The fish will be less likely to detect the hook and will feel little line resistance as it runs. When bobber-fishing, use the smallest float possible so the fish can swim off without feeling drag. Experiment to determine the right amount of time before you set the hook.

How to Hook Worms for Nibbling Panfish

THREAD the worm onto the shaft or hook the worm several times, leaving only a short section of the tail dangling. If fish continue to strike short, thread on the remainder of the tail.

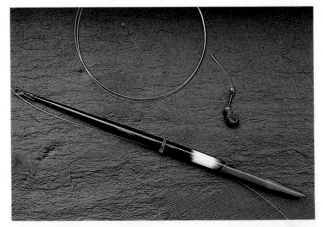

BAIT a #10 or #12 hook with a 1/4- to 1/2-inch piece of worm to catch nibbling sunfish. Use a quill bobber, Carolina float or other small, sensitive float. Set the hook the moment the bobber moves.

How to Fish a Standard Worm Harness

CAST or troll a worm harness for walleyes, bass or other large gamefish. Use a gold or silver blade when fishing clear water and a fluorescent blade for murky or bog-stained water. Hook the crawler so it trails naturally.

How to Tie a Threaded Worm Harness: The Snell Knot

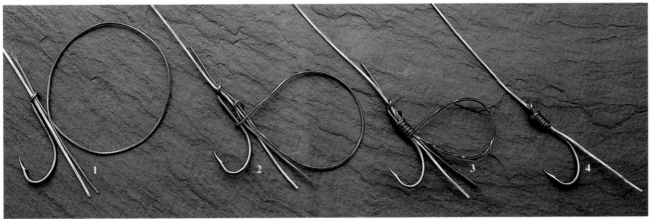

TIE a sliding snell by (1) threading the line through the eye of a #6 hook. Let 1 inch extend past the bend. Thread another piece of line through the eye and make a large loop. (2) Begin the snell by wrapping the front part of the loop around the line and the shaft. (3) Continue snelling until you complete six wraps around the shaft. (4) Snug up the snell by pulling both ends firmly. Trim the tag ends. (For illustration, heavy line is used.)

How to Tie a Threaded Worm Harness: Rigging the Worm

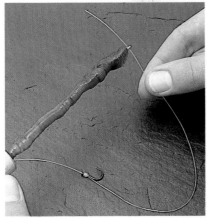  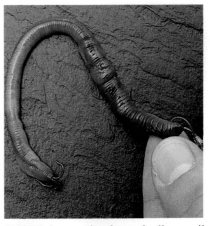

SLIDE a snelled hook up the line. Thread a crawler tail-first onto a needle stuck into a wooden dowel. Thread the line through the eye.

PULL the line back through the night-crawler so the end protrudes a few inches past the tail. Then tie on a #10 treble hook.

SLIDE the crawler down the line until it covers the treble hook shank. Then slide the snelled hook down and push it through the crawler's head.

Aquatic Insects

From warm, stagnant ponds to icy, fast-flowing streams, nearly every kind of freshwater habitat holds some insect life. Most insects eaten by fish live in the water. Called *aquatic insects,* they spend their egg and immature stages in water and their adult stage on land.

Immature insects, also called *larvae,* are wingless and have tiny gills. They live on stream or lake bottoms, where they are a source of food for fish.

The immature stage of mayflies, stoneflies, dragonflies and damselflies is called a *nymph;* for dobsonflies it is a *hellgrammite;* for crane flies a *waterworm;* and for caddisflies a *caddisworm.*

Insects feed and grow during the larval stage, which may last from a few days to several years. As the insect grows, it *molts,* or sheds its outer skin. Some species molt more than 40 times, some only four. The last molt produces a winged, mature adult.

Insects such as caddisflies and crane flies have a transitional stage between their larval and adult forms. Called a *pupa,* the insect lives in a cocoon-like case where it changes into an adult.

Mayfly and caddisfly adults hatch in water, while stonefly, dragonfly and damselfly larvae crawl onto land before emerging as adults. Insect hatches occur throughout the year. The largest hatches usually take place in warm weather and cause frenzied feeding among trout, bluegills and other fish.

Below is a diagram showing the life cycle for one type of mayfly. In this case the cycle spans one year. Life cycles vary from five weeks to two years among different mayfly species.

The major kinds of aquatic insects are described on pages 84 and 85. Fishermen use all of the immature forms as bait. Adults are seldom used for bait, with the exception of stoneflies and mayflies.

MAYFLY LIFE CYCLE begins with (1) a male and female mating in flight. (2) After mating, the female deposits her eggs. (3) The eggs sink, adhering to plants, rocks and debris. (4) The nymphs, or larvae, hatch in about six months. They feed and grow for about five months and undergo many molts. (5) When full-grown, the nymph swims to the surface, (6) where it splits and sheds its skin. In seconds, a newly-emerged *subimago* or *dun* hardens its wings, then flies off to nearby vegetation. (7) After a day or two, the dun molts into a mature insect called an *imago* or *spinner.* Some adults live just long enough to breed and lay eggs; others live for weeks.

STONEFLY NYMPHS have two tails and are ½ to 2 inches in length. They live among the rocks and gravel of cool streams for three months to three years, depending on the species.

ADULT STONEFLIES are dull-colored. The wings, which lie flat against the back, have a leathery appearance. The salmon fly (above) is a large species of stonefly that hatches in huge swarms on western streams.

MAYFLY NYMPHS usually have three tails. Most fishermen prefer the larger, inch-long nymphs found in muddy stream bottoms.

MAYFLY DUNS are winged, but still sexually immature. Most are dull-colored and have gray wings, though some species have mottled wings.

ADULT MAYFLIES, called spinners, have triangular wings that stand upright. The upturned tail may be three times as long as the body.

CADDISCASES are the homes of caddisworms. Made of rock or plant fragments, the ½- to 1½-inch cases are attached to underwater objects.

CADDISWORMS live about one year. The body is cream-colored with a dark head. They are usually ½ to ¾ inch in length.

ADULT CADDISFLIES have rooflike wings that cover the body. The drab brown or gray adults live less than one month.

WATERWORMS, or crane fly larvae, grow to 3 inches in length. They have a soft, wrinkled body and several hairy lobes on the tail. They live in leaf piles, beaver dams and debris on the stream bottom.

ADULT CRANE FLIES resemble overgrown mosquitoes. About 1 inch in length, they have long, spindly legs and veined wings. Crane flies are most abundant near tree-lined streambanks or damp woodlands.

HELLGRAMMITES, or dobsonfly larvae, live in rocky streams and in some large lakes. They have a tough, brown body and protruding jaws that can inflict a painful bite. Some species grow to 3 inches in length.

ADULT DOBSONFLIES are large; some types have a wingspread exceeding 5 inches. Their bodies may be black, brown or orange, and their wings are transparent. Lights often draw them far from water.

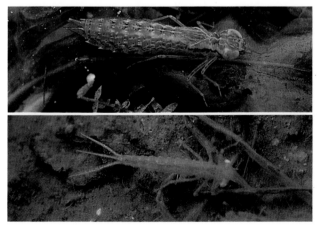

NYMPHS of dragonflies (top) and damselflies (bottom) are ½ to 1½ inches long. They vary in color from dark brown to pale green; some are thin and others nearly round. They live in debris in slow-moving water.

ADULT dragonflies (top) rest with wings extended; damselflies (bottom) hold their wings over their bodies. Both kinds are seen darting and hovering above streams, ponds, lakes and marshes.

Catching and Keeping Aquatic Insects

BEAVER DAMS are prime spots for collecting burrowing larvae such as mayfly nymphs and waterworms. Dig through silt, leaves and sticks.

Aquatic insects are convenient bait because you can collect them as you fish your way along a streambank or lakeshore. Any common insect larvae will usually catch fish.

Be alert for clues to help you find insects. Dobsonflies deposit their eggs in white, paint-like blotches on rocks and bridge pilings. The eggs fall into the water and hatch into hellgrammites within two

WATERWORMS are often found by digging through mud and leaves by hand. Look for the worms in silty deposits downstream from fallen trees.

Tips for Catching Aquatic Insect Larvae

LIFT a rock, then check for larvae on the underside. This is a good way to collect caddiscases, stonefly nymphs and other insect larvae.

SORT through mud, leaves and sticks near shore to find dragonfly and damselfly nymphs. A paint tray works well for picking out insects.

DIG in mud along a streambank to find mayfly nymphs. Make your own collecting tool by replacing the middle tines of a pitchfork with metal screen.

weeks. Look for these larvae under rocks downstream from the blotches. To find mayfly nymphs, search shallow, quiet waters along stream edges or lakeshores. Check mud bottoms for tiny burrows dug by the nymphs. Burrow openings are from ⅛ to ¼ inch in diameter.

When a hatch is on, look for adult insects on plants, bridge abutments or other objects near the water.

Aquatic insects do not have to be used immediately. Most will stay alive for several days or weeks if refrigerated or kept in aerated water. Many can be frozen and used months later. Mayfly and stonefly nymphs cannot be frozen because their insides turn to liquid, leaving only a loose skin. Freezing hellgrammites makes them soft and difficult to keep on the hook.

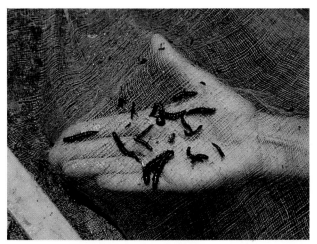

HELLGRAMMITES grab a cheesecloth net with their strong pinchers and are difficult to shake off. One person holds the net while another removes the insects.

KICK rocks to dislodge hellgrammites and other larvae. Let the current sweep the insects downstream. Gather them in a cheesecloth net stretched between two sticks.

How to Keep Aquatic Insect Larvae

PLACE the larvae in a small plastic container filled with damp leaves or moss. Put in only enough insects for a day's fishing. Refrigerate the larvae until you are ready to use them. Most kinds will live for several days.

AERATE a large container with an aquarium pump to keep larvae alive for an extended period. If possible, use water from the stream and keep it cool. Add clumps of moss or aquatic plants for cover.

Land Insects

A land or *terrestrial* insect completes each stage of its life cycle on dry ground. These insects fall prey to fish when they drop or wash into lakes or streams. Other land insects never seen by fish still make excellent bait.

Many land insects pass through egg, larval and adult stages. Others have a pupal stage in which the insect develops into an adult inside a cocoon. The catalpa worm, the larval stage of the catalpa sphinx moth, has a life cycle typical of many land insects. The adult moths emerge from pupae in spring and lay eggs on branches of catalpa trees. The eggs hatch and the larvae begin to feed on the leaves. When full-grown, the caterpillars crawl or drop to the ground, dig cells in the soil and form pupae. In about ten days, the adult moths emerge, mate and lay eggs. This cycle may be repeated several times

CRICKETS abound in woods and fields, especially the dark-colored field cricket (right). The gray cricket (left) is a house cricket that is raised commercially and sold in many bait shops and pet stores.

How to Identify Caterpillars

CATALPA worms grow to 3 inches in length. They have prominent black stripes down the back and a black, tail-like spine.

WAXWORMS, the larvae of wax or bee moths, are usually ½ to 1 inch long. The body is cream-colored with a darker head.

TENT CATERPILLARS are bluish-black with a light stripe down the back. The 2-inch body is covered with fine hairs.

How to Identify Maggots

GOLDENROD GRUBS are the larvae of goldenrod gall flies. The gallworm is whitish and about the size of a popcorn kernel.

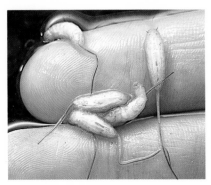

MOUSEES, or rat-tailed maggots, live in water, but the pale brown larvae breathe through a tail-like tube so they are considered land insects.

SILVER WIGGLERS, or *spikes*, are the larvae of flies such as the housefly and blowfly. About ½ inch long, they have an unpleasant smell.

during summer. When the weather cools, the pupae become dormant until the following spring.

Following are the common types of larval and adult insects used by bait fishermen:

CATERPILLARS. Many kinds of butterfly and moth larvae are used for bait, including catalpa worms, waxworms, tent caterpillars, webworms, leaf rollers, corn earworms and cutworms.

MAGGOTS. Fly larvae, or maggots, are most popular among ice fishermen. Favorites are silver wigglers, goldenrod grubs and mousees.

GRUBS. Beetle larvae, or grubs, make excellent panfish bait. Mealworms, white grubs and acorn grubs are the most commonly used.

WASP AND SAWFLY LARVAE. Anglers sometimes use larvae of wasps, bees and hornets. These larvae are effective baits, but many fishermen are reluctant to gather them. Sawflies resemble hornets. Their larvae are also used for bait.

ADULT INSECTS. Crickets and grasshoppers are the most widely used. Fishermen also use cockroaches, moths, wasps and bees.

GRASSHOPPERS thrive in grassy or weedy fields. Most are 1 to 2 inches long. Grasshoppers that live on the ground are usually some shade of gray or brown; those that live on plants are often green.

How to Identify Grubs

MEALWORMS, or *golden grubs,* are the larvae of darkling beetles. About 1 inch long, they vary from yellow to brown with darker heads.

WHITE GRUBS are larvae of June bugs and other scarab beetles. The 1-inch body is crescent-shaped and white with a darker head.

ACORN GRUBS, the larvae of acorn and nut weevils, are seldom longer than ¼ inch. They are cream-colored and resemble goldenrod grubs.

How to Identify Wasp and Sawfly Larvae

PAPER WASP LARVAE are plump, off-white in color and up to 1 inch long. Their gray-colored hives often hang from eaves of buildings. One hive usually produces dozens of larvae.

ELM SAWFLY LARVAE are ¾ to 1½ inches long. The different species vary from pale green to yellow, but all have a dark stripe down the back. They are found on elm and willow trees in late spring and summer.

Catching and Keeping Crickets and Grasshoppers

HOLD up a fuzzy wool blanket. Face into the wind while another person runs through the grass to scare up grasshoppers. The insects will sail with the wind and land on the blanket, where their legs become entangled.

Crickets and grasshoppers have remarkable leaping ability and seem to sense just when someone is about to grab them. But catching these insects is easy if you use the methods shown on these pages.

You can catch crickets and grasshoppers by hand, but you must choose the right time. Insects move more slowly as the temperature drops. Collect them when the air is cool, such as in early morning or on a rainy day. Some fishermen use flashlights to spot grasshoppers and crickets at night.

You may want to transfer the insects from the collecting container into smaller containers. To slow them down, place the insects in a refrigerator for 10 to 15 minutes before handling.

When keeping live crickets or grasshoppers, give them plenty of room in a cool container. Add grass for cover. The insects can also be frozen and used months later. Once thawed, their bodies soften, making them more appealing to some fish. They cannot be refrozen because they become too soft to keep on the hook.

Tips for Keeping Crickets and Grasshoppers

KEEP insects in a small screen box. This container is made of thin wood and window screen. It has a sliding door with a rubber slit.

OPEN the door to remove an insect. Rubber bands snap the door shut, keeping it tightly closed after the insect is removed.

CUT a tab near the edge of a coffee can lid so it opens at the rim. To remove an insect, push in the tab and shake until one comes out.

Tips for Catching Crickets

TURN OVER logs, stones or boards to catch crickets in fields or woods. To keep the crickets from escaping, surround them with a piece of stovepipe or cardboard.

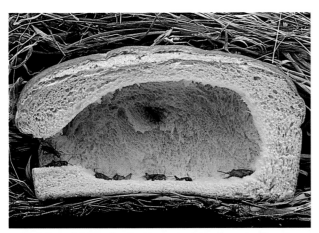

HOLLOW OUT a loaf of bread with a long knife. Cut a small hole near the bottom of one end. Place the loaf trap (cross section) in straw or weeds and leave it overnight. Collect crickets from the trap the next morning.

BURY a coffee can (cross section) baited with bread crumbs and sugar. Place small rocks around the rim, then cover the can with a board to keep rain out. Crickets enter between the rocks. Check the trap the next morning.

CARRY crickets in a commercial insect container. Crickets funnel into a small compartment. Turn the top until the opening lines up with an insect. Grab the cricket when it appears.

STORE crickets and grasshoppers in a container with air holes in the cover. Each day, add a damp paper towel for moisture and a small amount of corn meal. If stored in a cool area, the insects will stay alive for several weeks.

Collecting and Keeping Land Insect Larvae

Many bait shops sell mealworms, waxworms, goldenrod grubs and the larvae of other land insects, especially in northern states where these baits are popular among ice fishermen. But the supplies of bait dealers can become depleted quickly when fish are biting.

Some fishermen collect their own insect larvae. Others raise the larvae, removing what they need for fishing, but leaving enough breeders to insure a constant supply.

The larvae of most insects can be kept alive for several weeks or months. Remove dead ones periodically so they do not contaminate the others.

Some larvae can be frozen for later use. Goldenrod grubs should be frozen while still inside their galls and acorn grubs inside the acorns. Catalpa worms retain much of their original texture and color if frozen in water, but turn soft if frozen dry. It is not advisable to freeze larvae of most other insects because they turn black and become soft.

How to Collect and Keep Catalpa Worms

CATALPA WORMS feed on the leaves of catalpa trees beginning in late spring and continuing into early fall. Look for trees with large, heart-shaped leaves.

SHAKE worms off the leaves onto a blanket spread beneath the tree. Or pick the worms off the leaves, either from the ground or from a stepladder.

KEEP the worms in a moist burlap bag filled with fresh leaves. Avoid placing them in direct sunlight. The worms can be kept several weeks in a refrigerator.

How to Collect and Keep Waxworms

WAXWORMS tunnel into wax cells in beehives. Look for them in the cells or lying in debris on the bottom of the hive. Ask a beekeeper for help in locating stored or neglected beehives. Waxworms are considered pests because they feed on beeswax. Keep the worms in wood shavings in a dark place at room temperature.

How to Raise Waxworms

MIX 14 oz. cornflakes, 6 oz. brewer's yeast, 2 oz. grated beeswax. In another bowl, combine 6 oz. glycerine, 7 oz. honey, 3 oz. water. Mix all ingredients until moist.

PLACE the mixture in a 2-quart jar. Add one or two dozen waxworms. Cover the jar with mesh and keep in a dark place. The worms will burrow into the mixture.

ADD pleated wax paper after the larvae come to the surface to spin their cocoons. Adult moths will hatch from the cocoons and lay eggs on the paper.

TRANSFER the paper and eggs to another jar containing the same mixture. Larvae will hatch in about one week. Remove the larvae when they reach bait size.

How to Collect and Keep Mealworms

SIFT through piles of rotting grain around elevators, farms and feed mills to find mealworms. Pick them out by hand or use a sieve or fine-mesh net.

KEEP mealworms in containers with wood shavings, cornmeal or bran. They can be kept in a refrigerator for up to 6 months.

How to Collect and Keep Goldenrod Galls

GATHER galls on goldenrod plants in woodlands, meadows and fields from late fall to spring.

AVOID galls with holes. Birds have pecked out the larvae, or the worms have tunneled from the galls.

SLICE the gall lengthwise or crosswise. The cut should be shallow to avoid damaging the worm.

How to Collect and Keep Other Land Insect Larvae

TENT CATERPILLARS build silky, tent-like nests in tree branches from spring to mid-summer. Webworms are similar but are found in fall. Keep the larvae cool and feed them leaves from the host tree.

WHITE GRUBS can be collected by digging in black dirt, especially where there are chunks of rotting wood. Keep them in loose, slightly damp soil. If kept cool, they will stay alive for weeks.

94

How to Raise Mealworms

DROP about 100 mealworms into a bucket of bran or chicken mash. Each day, add a potato slice for moisture.

ADD crumpled paper towels. Larvae hide in the toweling, form pupae and later emerge as adult beetles.

TRANSFER beetles to a bucket of flour where they will lay eggs. Remove the new larvae in a few weeks.

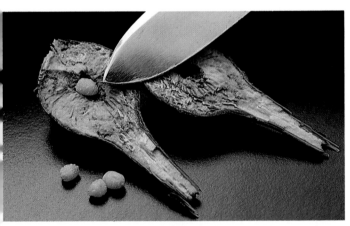

PRY open the gall with your thumbs. A knife or heavy scissors may be needed to open hard galls. Refrigerate the grubs in bran, oatmeal or cornmeal.

FREEZE or refrigerate unopened galls. Refrigerated, they will stay alive for months; frozen, they will keep up to two years.

ACORN GRUBS are found in acorns with tiny holes. Collect acorns just after they fall. Refrigerate them for several months, or freeze up to one year.

MOUSEES can be netted in livestock runoff or cannery discharges. Keep them at room temperature in a small container with wood shavings.

ELM SAWFLY LARVAE feed on elm and willow leaves from late spring to early summer. They can be refrigerated for several weeks.

Fishing With Insects

Many fishermen rate insects among the best live baits, especially for trout and panfish. Yet insects are not as widely used as worms and minnows because only a few kinds are regularly sold at bait shops. In most cases, anglers must collect their own.

Anglers have many misconceptions about insects as bait. Some trout fishermen believe they must match the hatch to catch fish. While trout sometimes feed solely on one type of hatching insect, this is generally not the case. A trout is likely to grab any insect that drifts by. Fly fishermen know that trout will strike a grasshopper imitation even when a hatch of mayflies or other aquatic insect is in progress.

Some fishermen believe that insects catch only small fish. But many anglers have found the stomachs of trophy smallmouth bass, trout and walleyes stuffed with insect larvae. Even after feeding, a big fish will sometimes grab an insect.

Another common misbelief is that insects will not catch fish when streams are high and muddy. Although fish have difficulty seeing insects floating on the surface of murky water, they can quickly detect an insect drifted along bottom.

The effectiveness of insects is largely due to their scent. This explains why plastic insect imitations never work as well as the real thing. An insect hooked through the body so its fluids seep into the water will often catch more fish than an insect hooked through the head. Some fishermen freeze insects, which softens the body so it releases more scent. After a short time, water will wash away most of the scent, so it pays to change bait frequently.

Small, fragile-bodied insects are difficult to hook and to fish naturally. Most anglers use light-wire hooks. A heavy hook will weigh down the insect and tear its body. Unless you use the proper hooking method, the insect will fall off when cast or be stolen by fish.

It is not necessary to hook an insect through the head or near the front of the body. Many insects will stay on the hook longer if threaded through the tail and out behind the head. Hooked this way, the insect will be retrieved tail-first, but this does not seem to keep fish from striking.

Use a slow retrieve when fishing in still water. Fish are not used to seeing insects move quickly. In a stream, let the insect float with the current. Many fishermen use line as light as 2-pound test so the insect will drift naturally. Light line is also less likely to spook fish. In streams, dead insects work almost as well as live ones because the fish do not have as much time to inspect the bait.

Most fishermen use light spinning tackle to cast a nearly weightless insect. Some prefer fly rods with floating lines to drift adult insects on the surface. Others use long cane poles to drop insects into hard-to-reach spots and to prevent snapping them off the line when casting. Whatever the tackle, set the hook at the first sign of a bite. Fish generally swallow an insect quickly.

Insects *continued*

Trout

Every stream fisherman has thrilled to the sight of trout dimpling the surface during an insect hatch. Insects make up a large part of the diet of most trout. Some species, such as the cutthroat, eat insects almost exclusively.

Most anglers assume that dimpling trout are feeding on adult insects. They try to duplicate the hatching

insect with an artificial fly, or they collect adult insects and float them on the surface. But few fishermen realize that trout feed more heavily on nymphs below the surface during a hatch. If you can find the larvae of the hatching insect, you will probably catch more trout. Larvae also stay on the hook better and can be cast farther.

Adult insects can also be effective when fished below the surface. Grasshoppers, mayflies and stoneflies drifted in mid-water or along a stream bottom catch many more trout than adult insects floated on the surface.

Under most conditions, trout are not choosy about the insects they eat because food is not that plentiful. But when a large insect hatch is in progress, trout become more selective. Food is so abundant they ignore everything except the specific insect that is hatching.

GRASSHOPPERS can be hooked under the collar, threaded lengthwise so the hook protrudes from the tail, or threaded so the hook emerges from the collar or just ahead of it. Use a #6 to #10 light-wire hook.

DRAGONFLY NYMPHS should be hooked just under the collar with a #8 or #10 light-wire hook. Thread the smaller damselfly nymph (not shown) on a #10 or #12 long-shank hook.

HELLGRAMMITES live longer if hooked just under the collar with a #4 to #8 hook. But they stay on better if threaded. Hold them behind the head to avoid the pinchers.

MAYFLY NYMPHS (right) should be hooked through the hard plate just behind the head. Hook the adult mayfly through the head. Use a #10 or #12 light-wire hook.

STONEFLY NYMPHS (right) are hooked through the collar with a #8 or #10 light-wire hook. The more fragile adult should be hooked through the head with a #10 or #12 hook.

WATERWORMS should be hooked through the tough skin just ahead of the tail lobes. Use a #8 or #10 light-wire hook.

PEEL apart a caddiscase to expose the larva. Grasp the worm, then pull slowly and steadily until it loosens its grip on the case.

CADDISWORMS are hooked in the head or threaded on a #12 to #16 light-wire hook. Some anglers use several worms, or the worm and case.

Tips for Fishing Trout With Insects

FLOAT an insect on the stream surface with a floating fly line. Feed line as the bait drifts downstream. Or gently lob the bait, then retrieve in short twitches.

AVOID drag. The insect should float at the same speed as the current. If it floats faster or slower, it creates a *V* on the surface and appears unnatural.

DRIFT a split-shot rig along bottom. Cast upstream and allow the insect to tumble with the current. Reel up slack as the bait drifts.

TIE a casting bubble rig by threading on the bubble; add a barrel swivel and a 4- to 6-foot leader. The bubble adds weight but will not spook fish.

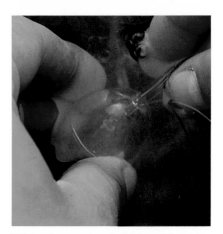

FILL the casting bubble with water for extra casting distance. When filled, the bubble sinks, carrying the bait to the fish in deep water.

How to Fish an Insect Hatch

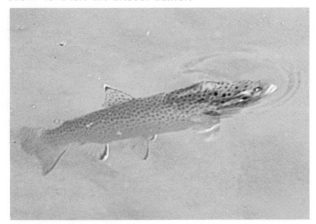

LOOK for rings or dimples on the surface caused by trout feeding on hatching insects. Hatches usually occur in late afternoon and early evening, beginning in spring and continuing through summer.

LOB an insect larva using a sinking-tip fly line. In moving water, let the insect drift with the current. In still water, retrieve in short twitches. Or use a water-filled casting bubble and spinning gear.

Panfish

Fishermen who have heard sunfish slurping bugs off the surface on a warm summer evening know that panfish like insects.

Southern anglers rate crickets among the top baits for sunfish, or *bream*. Fishermen in the North regularly use land insect larvae for ice fishing, but seldom try them in warm weather. Many anglers are now discovering that waxworms, mealworms and other larvae popular for ice fishing work just as well in summer.

Insects attract panfish by scent. So instead of using a caterpillar in its natural state, turn it inside out to release more body juices into the water. Rather than hooking one larva to look natural, put several on the hook. And instead of replacing larvae mangled by a biting fish, leave them on when you add fresh bait.

Anglers have found that panfish will also bite on aquatic insect larvae, especially during a hatch. Then crappies may ignore minnows and chase mayfly nymphs or other larvae wiggling toward the surface.

How to Hook Insects

CRICKETS and grasshoppers are threaded on #8 light-wire hooks. Some anglers remove the legs to make the bait look smaller.

NYMPHS of dragonflies, mayflies, stoneflies and other insects can be hooked on small jigs or on a plain hook (page 99).

LAND INSECT LARVAE, such as (left to right) waxworms, mealworms and silver wigglers, are often fished with artificial flies or teardrops.

How to Rig a Catalpa Worm Inside Out

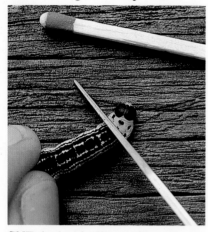

CUT the head off a catalpa worm or other caterpillar with a sharp knife. Slice large caterpillars in half.

PUSH a matchstick into the uncut end to turn the worm inside out. Carefully withdraw the matchstick.

PIERCE the catalpa worm through the middle with a #6 hook. Scent from the body fluids attracts panfish.

How to Catch Panfish With Insects

SLOW-TROLL a ⅛- or ¼-ounce slip-sinker rig or split-shot rig. Look for deep, sandy or rocky shoals to find rock bass, sunfish, crappies or yellow perch.

CAST parallel to a weedline using a small bobber, split-shot and an insect larva. Retrieve the bobber with twitches followed by pauses. Panfish swim out of the weeds to grab the insect.

DROP an insect larva hooked on a teardrop, small jig or plain hook into a pocket in the vegetation. Use a Carbonyte® float or other sensitive bobber. Let the insect rest a few seconds, then drop it into a different pocket.

Ice Fishing

A tiny insect larva is often the ideal ice-fishing bait, especially for panfish. Insects also work well for rainbows and other stream trout in ice-bound lakes. Crappie and perch anglers prefer minnows but switch to insects when fishing is slow. Most fishermen tip a small fly, jig or teardrop with insect larvae. Some thread one or more larvae on a plain hook.

In winter, when fish are less active, they may take an insect without moving the float. To solve this problem, attach a *spring-bobber* to your ice-fishing rod. The sensitive spring allows you to detect bites more easily and to change depths without adjusting a bobber. Anglers can make their own spring-bobbers or purchase them at most bait shops.

PANFISH BAITS include (1) goldenrod grubs on teardrop jig, (2) silver wiggler on artificial ant, (3) waxworm on teardrop, (4) mayfly nymph on homemade willowleaf spoon. Mousees and mealworms are also popular.

LARGE SUNFISH feed actively just before ice-out, when melt-water honeycombs the ice. Sunfish also bite well for several weeks after freeze-up. Check the ice thickness carefully in the area you plan to fish.

How to Make and Use a Spring-bobber

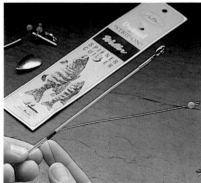

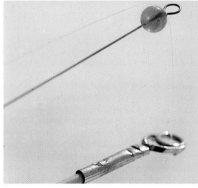

REMOVE all hardware from a strip-on spinner. Slide one bead to the end of the wire; wrap the other end to the rod with winding thread.

THREAD 4-pound mono through the eye in the wire and then through the rod tip. Attach a teardrop jig baited with an insect larva.

JIG the bait, then pause for a few seconds to wait for a bite. If the spring twitches or stops moving as you raise the rod, set the hook.

Bass

Expert stream fishermen know that smallmouths like hellgrammites nearly as well as they like crayfish. Hellgrammites will stay alive for hours and can be cast repeatedly without tearing off the hook. Other good smallmouth baits include crickets, grasshoppers and any of the larger aquatic insect larvae. Most smallmouths are caught by drifting insects along bottom. Floating a grasshopper or cricket on the surface will also work.

Jumbo grasshoppers or hellgrammites may work well for largemouth bass in summer, but fishermen seldom use other insects for largemouths.

How to Fish Grasshoppers for Largemouths

THREAD a jumbo grasshopper onto a #4 or #6 long-shank hook. Use a 2- to 3-inch grasshopper. Attach a small bobber to dangle the insect near heavy cover.

BIG SMALLMOUTHS can be caught on hellgrammites and other aquatic insect larvae. These baits work because a smallmouth eats insects as part of its natural diet.

How to Fish Insects for Smallmouth Bass

PUSH a #4 or #6 hook just under the collar of a large hellgrammite. Thread a #8 or #10 long-shank hook through the body of a cricket. Add split-shot.

CAST a hellgrammite into a riffle and let it drift into the downstream pool. Hungry smallmouths feed in the fast water in morning and evening.

FLOAT a cricket using a plastic bubble or floating fly line. When the insect becomes water-logged and begins to sink, replace it with a fresh one.

Catfish & Bullheads

Insects may seem an unlikely bait for catfish, but there are times when they work better than any other bait. Catfish change their food preferences several times throughout the year. Fishermen must constantly experiment to determine which baits work best. Insects such as grasshoppers, catalpa worms and mayflies are sometimes more effective than other well-known catfish baits.

When digging for worms, bullhead fishermen sometimes find white grubs. Some anglers claim the grubs work as well as worms. Other types of grubs and wasp larvae are also good bullhead baits.

How to Rig White Grubs for Bullheads

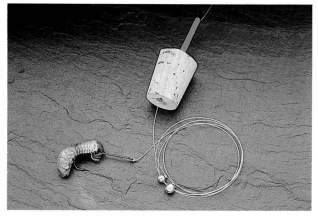

HOOK a white grub lengthwise through the body. Use a #2 or #4 long-shank hook. Fish the grub on bottom or use a bobber to float it just off bottom.

CATFISH detect the smell of catalpa worms and other baits using taste sensors located around their mouths and in their whiskers, or barbels.

How to Rig Insects for Catfish

CATALPA WORMS are hooked in the middle of the body with #1 or #2 hooks. Use a slip-sinker rig or trotline (page 47). Some fishermen use several worms or turn worms inside out (page 102) for extra scent.

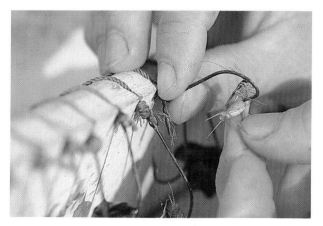

GRASSHOPPERS should be threaded onto trotline hooks to prevent small fish from stealing the bait. Or fish hoppers with a slip-sinker rig. Catfish prefer jumbo hoppers from 2 to 3 inches long.

Salamanders

Generations of fishermen in the southeastern states have used salamanders for bait. Salamanders are gaining popularity in other parts of the country. They are lively, durable baits that are especially attractive to large gamefish.

Salamanders are unusual among cold-blooded animals because they are more active when temperatures are cool. In cold weather, salamanders that live on land hibernate by burrowing into soil or plant debris. Those that live in water lie dormant on bottom.

Because they absorb moisture through their skin, salamanders and other *amphibians* must live either in water or in damp places. The skin of most amphibians contains a mucous that is mildly toxic to warm-blooded animals but not offensive to fish.

More than 100 species of salamanders live in North America. Southeastern states have the greatest variety, although many kinds are found in other regions of the United States, and in Canada and Mexico.

Nearly every species of salamander is used for bait. The most commonly used fall into three groups:

MOLE SALAMANDERS. Named for their habit of burrowing into damp soil, these thick-bodied salamanders seldom come out except on rainy nights. In spring, they migrate to shallow ponds to breed and lay eggs. The larvae live in water and gradually change into land-dwelling adults.

The tiger salamander is the most common mole salamander. Its larvae are called *waterdogs* by fishermen, but this term is confusing because true waterdogs are actually members of the giant salamander group. Throughout this book, the term waterdog refers to the larval tiger salamander rather than the true waterdog. It is difficult to tell the difference between the larvae of tiger salamanders and those of other mole salamanders. So fishermen sometimes use the term waterdog for any mole salamander larvae.

GIANT SALAMANDERS. These salamanders, including sirens, mudpuppies and *true* waterdogs, live in water all of their lives. They prefer shallow, stagnant water.

LUNGLESS SALAMANDERS. Often called *spring lizards*, these salamanders live along the edges of cold springs, brooks or streams. Some types live in cool, moist woodlands. Spring lizards have sleek bodies and most are excellent swimmers.

MOLE SALAMANDERS vary from 2 to 9 inches. Most have thick legs and spots or stripes. They are found throughout the United States, into southern Canada and northern Mexico. Shown is the tiger salamander.

GIANT SALAMANDERS have external gills. Mud-puppies (above) and true waterdogs have four legs and are similar in appearance. True waterdogs reach 9 inches and are found only in Atlantic and Gulf Coast states. Mudpuppies grow to 13 inches and live in the eastern half of the country, excluding coastal states.

SIRENS, another type of giant salamander, range from 6 to 30 inches. They have tiny front legs and no hind legs. Color varies from black to olive-green. Sirens are found in the south central and southeastern states.

LUNGLESS SALAMANDERS grow to 8 inches. Many have large hind legs. They thrive in the Appalachians but are found in the eastern half of the United States into Canada. Shown is the black-bellied salamander.

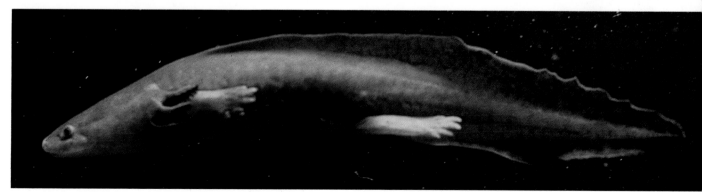

LARVAL TIGER SALAMANDERS, or waterdogs, are 4 to 8 inches long. They have external gills and four partially-developed legs. A long, continuous fin extends around the rear half of the body. The larvae spend their first few months in water. Eventually they lose their gills, grow strong legs and begin moving about on land. Waterdogs are harvested from natural ponds or raised commercially in artificial ponds.

Catching and Keeping Salamanders

Mole salamanders are abundant and easy to find in spring, especially after the season's first rains. Look for them at night in open areas near ponds. Later in the year, mole salamanders scatter and become solitary. Once they burrow into the soil, they are nearly impossible to find. A few can be collected from rock piles near breeding ponds. Waterdogs can be seined or netted from the same ponds.

Many kinds of spring lizards live under moss or rotting logs along the edges of cool-water streams, brooks and springs. Woodland types live under debris on the forest floor. These salamanders hide during the day but may come out in rainy weather. They are most easily found as they move about at night. Catching spring lizards can be difficult because they move quickly.

Giant salamanders live in the shallows of lakes, in canals, and in backwaters and other slow-moving areas of rivers. Collectors often catch mudpuppies and true waterdogs on hook and line, using worms for bait. After heavy rains, sirens move into ditches connecting lakes and marshes, where they can be netted or caught in unbaited minnow traps.

Salamanders are one of the easiest baits to keep alive. Some anglers feed them worms or minnows, but salamanders will live for months without food.

LIFT rocks or other objects that cover cool, damp soil to find mole salamanders. They move slowly and are easy to grab.

SEINE small ponds to catch larval mole salamanders. The best ponds are temporary, usually drying up by mid-summer. They lack predatory fish that would quickly eat the larval salamanders.

SHAKE the roots of water hyacinth over a screen box to gather bait-size sirens. In weedless lakes or ponds, rake bottom debris onto shore and gather the sirens. Use a long-handled net to catch sirens around ditch culverts.

HAUL a seine along sheltered lakeshores or in river backwaters to capture mudpuppies and true waterdogs.

Look for areas with sparse weeds. Salamanders in dense stands of vegetation are difficult to seine.

SHINE a headlamp over rocks in a small stream to find spring lizards at night. Approaching too close scares them into the water. Catch them with a long-handled dip net.

Or, straighten a coat hanger, then bend it at a right angle 1/8 inch from the tip. Thread on a worm so the tail dangles; lift quickly when the salamander bites.

REFRIGERATE mole salamanders and spring lizards at about 45°F in a container with moist leaves or moss. Keep the cover secure but not airtight. Mole salamanders can also be refrigerated in loose, damp soil.

STORE larval salamanders, mudpuppies and true water-dogs in 50°F water. Change the water once a week. Keep sirens at room temperature. To prevent sirens from escaping, keep them in a half-filled bucket of water.

Frogs & Toads

Years ago, frogs were one of the most popular baits. Although they are still effective, frogs are not as widely used among today's fishermen. Frog populations in many regions have declined due to pesticides, disease and wetland drainage. Some states now restrict their harvest, but frogs can still be found in most areas.

Anglers use many kinds of frogs and toads as bait. Those pictured are the most commonly used.

Like salamanders, frogs and toads absorb oxygen and moisture through their skin and hibernate in winter. Toads burrow into the soil, while frogs dig into the muddy bottoms of lakes and deep ponds.

The larvae of frogs and toads, called *tadpoles*, hatch in the water. They have gills, tiny mouths and long tails. Tadpoles begin changing into frogs when they are about two months old. Most bullfrogs remain in the tadpole stage for two years. Although eaten by fish, tadpoles are too delicate to use as bait.

Leopard frogs are the most common type of frog and the most popular among fishermen. Sometimes called *meadow frogs*, they often wander into grassy fields. Pickerel frogs resemble leopard frogs, but their spots are square instead of round. Pickerel frogs reach only 3 inches in length from the tip of the snout to the tailbone. They live throughout the eastern half of the country.

Green frogs are popular among fishermen in the eastern half of the country. They are normally found in marshlands but may live along streams.

Bullfrogs are the largest species of frog. They prefer deeper water than most other frogs, and inhabit lakes, bayous, and deep ponds. If they cannot find this kind of habitat, they will live in streams, ponds or even marshes. Pig frogs and river frogs are almost identical to bullfrogs and live in similar habitat. Pig frogs have pointed snouts, while river frogs are dark with white spots on their lips. Both types are found in the southeastern United States. All these large frogs are generally used as cut-bait.

To identify the frogs pictured, look at their backs. Most have paired folds of skin, or *ridges*. Frogs cannot be identified by color because frogs of the same species may differ. Leopard frogs from the same pond may vary from light green to brown. Some have many spots; others have only a few.

LEOPARD FROGS are found throughout North America, excluding the Pacific Coast. They have ridges that run the length of the back and distinct, rounded spots. They grow to 4 inches long.

BULLFROGS reach 6 inches in length. They have a skin fold around the eardrum, and green to brown backs that lack ridges. Bullfrogs have light-colored undersides mottled with gray or brown. They are found throughout the United States, except in the northern plains and Rocky Mountain regions.

GREEN FROGS grow to 3½ inches. Ridges extend from the eye two-thirds of the way down the back. Their range includes the eastern half of the United States and southeastern Canada. Color varies from pale green to brown.

AMERICAN TOADS may reach 3½ inches. All have warty, dry skin and horizontal eye pupils, and most are dull brown. They are found in the eastern half of the United States and Canada.

Catching Frogs and Toads

In summer, tadpoles lose their tails, develop large mouths and grow legs. All tadpoles in a pond undergo this change at about the same time. Soon the shore is teeming with young frogs and a fisherman walking the water's edge can collect dozens. But within a few days, the frogs scatter and become more difficult to find. Leopard frogs, for example, disperse to other lakes and ponds, and to wet meadows. In fall, they migrate to deeper lakes and ponds, where they hibernate. In spring, they return to shallow waters where they breed and lay eggs.

Fishermen catch leopard, pickerel and green frogs by hand or with dip nets. Likely spots include marshy areas and the edges of streams or creeks. In fall, look for leopard frogs at night along roads separating marshes and lakes. When grabbing a frog, hold on firmly. It will often relax completely until you loosen your grip, then suddenly leap away.

Bullfrogs, pig frogs and river frogs spend most of their time in aquatic vegetation near deep water. Bullfrogs and pig frogs are more difficult to approach than river frogs. These frogs are easiest to find at night, using lights.

Collect these large frogs by netting, angling or spearing. *Gigs,* or spears, are 3 to 5 inches wide, with three to six barbed tines mounted on a long handle. Speared frogs are used as cut-bait.

CATCH a bullfrog or other large frog on a small, brightly-colored yarn fly. Use a cane pole, light monofilament and a #10 hook. The best time is after dusk.

NET frogs from the bow of a boat poled through shoreline weedbeds. Shining a light in a frog's eyes makes it easier to approach and capture.

GRAB toads near outdoor lights, where they gather to feed on insects just after dark. Warm summer nights are the best times to find toads.

Keeping Frogs and Toads

Frogs are not as easy to keep as most other baits. They require ample space, fresh water, food, places to hide, and platforms for resting and drying. If all these needs are met, frogs can be kept for months. If not, they become stressed and subject to disease. Reddish blotches may develop on the undersides of frogs held in captivity. Called *redleg,* this condition is a sure sign that frogs are under stress.

Containers for keeping frogs should have an air hole or be made of styrofoam or other porous material. To keep frogs from leaping out, use a deep container or one with a small hole in the cover. Staple a piece of inner tube over the hole. Slit the rubber so you can reach into the container to grab frogs. When keeping large frogs in open buckets, add enough water so they cannot get leverage to jump out.

During the first few days of captivity, frogs will jump against the sides of the container whenever they are disturbed. To keep frogs in good condition, line a cooler or screen box with a soft mesh, such as nylon seine material.

Feed frogs live crickets or other insects about three times a week. Provide them with bricks, broken clay pots or floating boards for resting and hiding spots. Frogs should be kept at room temperature or slightly cooler. They will dehydrate quickly and die if left out of water in hot weather.

COOLERS can be used to store frogs. Add an inch of water and pieces of broken clay pots. Change the water once a week. Discard frogs that appear unhealthy.

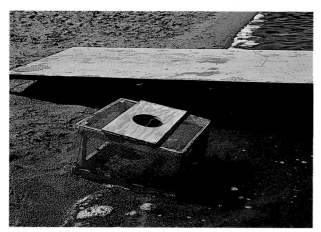

LIVE BOXES at water's edge provide frogs with fresh water and live insects. Place boards on one side and part of the top to protect frogs from sun and waves.

FROG BOXES are easy to transport and take up little space in a boat. Dunk the box occasionally and keep it out of the hot sun.

Fishing With Salamanders & Frogs

A frog kicking across the surface or a salamander twisting and turning on a hook makes an easy target for a gamefish.

Frogs have been a popular bait for decades. Although salamanders have long been used in southeastern states, they are not widely used elsewhere. But waterdogs are gaining a reputation as an excellent live bait, especially for large gamefish.

Most fishermen think of frogs as bait for largemouth bass. Frogs also work well for walleyes and northern pike. In the North, walleyes and northerns move inshore to feed about the same time leopard frogs arrive along lakeshores to hibernate. When the fish begin feeding on frogs, shore fishermen can catch a limit quickly. Other fish commonly caught on frogs include smallmouth bass and catfish.

Many fishermen consider salamanders a better bait than frogs. Salamanders stay alive longer and swim more actively when hooked. The most effective types are waterdogs, spring lizards and sirens, although any salamander will catch fish.

Waterdogs have become popular throughout the country. They are widely available at bait shops and can even be purchased through the mail. They work best for largemouth bass, walleyes and catfish. After waterdogs change into adult salamanders, they do not work as well.

Spring lizards are used to catch largemouth and smallmouth bass in the Southeast and are sold at many bait shops and roadside stands.

Sirens are one of the hardiest natural baits and have a unique, snake-like action. Anglers who use sirens claim they outfish other salamanders. They are used mainly for largemouth bass. Bait shops seldom carry sirens, so fishermen must catch their own.

Fishing with frogs and salamanders presents some special problems. Although you can keep them alive for long periods, they are not as durable on the hook as one might expect. Repeatedly casting a frog or salamander will soon kill it.

Hooking a fish can be difficult when using frogs and salamanders because fish sometimes strike the tail-end of the bait. To overcome this problem, attach a stinger hook to a hind leg or the tail.

When casting or trolling, the hook may wear a hole in the soft nose of a frog or salamander. Before long, the hook falls out. To keep the bait hooked, fishermen use bait-saver tabs punched out of plastic coffee can lids. Various types of harnesses are also used. Super Hooks™ are popular because they keep the bait alive. Instead of piercing the flesh, the hook is pinched on just behind the head. Small barbs on the inside surface of the hook hold the bait firmly between the twin shanks.

Largemouth Bass

For many years, spring lizards were a well-kept secret among a few bass fishermen in the southeastern United States. The popularity of spring lizards has spread throughout the eastern states and into southern Canada.

Fishermen in other areas of the country have discovered that largemouths prefer salamanders over most other baits. In an aquarium test, bass frequently ignored minnows, frogs and worms, but immediately grabbed a waterdog or spring lizard.

Almost every type of salamander will catch bass. An 8- to 10-inch larval salamander is one of the best baits for trophy bass. Some fishermen use 4- to 6-inch adult salamanders.

Sirens account for many big bass in the South. The sirens swim with an enticing motion and are more active than larval salamanders.

Frogs have been a traditional bass bait for decades. Fishermen can choose from hundreds of lures that resemble frogs. Anglers still use frogs in many areas, but salamanders have become more popular.

How to Fish a Bait-saver Rig

THREAD a cone sinker on the line. Add a #4 hook, then force a bait-saver tab down the shank. Hook a salamander through both lips. Add another plastic tab, then push the tabs against the bait.

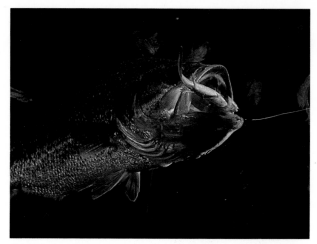

CAST the bait, then let it settle. Retrieve by lifting quickly. Bass usually strike as the salamander sinks. The sliding cone sinker improves feel and slips easily through weeds. In heavy cover, use a weedless hook.

Other Salamander Rigs

PUSH a #2 hook through the back of a 6- to 8-inch siren. With a free line, the siren will swim toward bottom, seeking cover in weeds, brush, trees or other places where largemouth bass are likely to be found.

HOOK a spring lizard just ahead of the back leg. Using a #2 or #4 hook with a split-shot or light slip-sinker rig, cast and slowly retrieve the bait. Some anglers still-fish on bottom or suspend the bait with a bobber.

How to Fish With Frogs

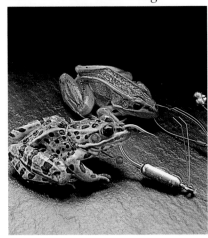

TIE a #4 weedless hook or a hook-harness to 20-pound mono. Hook the frog through both lips from the bottom; add split-shot if needed.

DROP the frog into a pocket in the weeds with a stout cane pole. Work one pocket for a few minutes, then drop the frog into another.

HOIST the bass from the weeds as quickly as possible. If you allow the fish to run, it may tangle in the weeds and break free.

Catfish

During the hottest weeks of summer, the whereabouts of giant catfish are a mystery to most fishermen. The usual bottom-fishing techniques may continue to produce small channel cats, or *fiddlers*, but few trophy flatheads or blues.

Along large rivers, catfish experts have found that the biggest fish frequently suspend during midsummer. They congregate in deep eddies, sometimes far above bottom. To catch these monstrous fish, some anglers use a large sliding float to keep the bait at the right depth. A live frog or salamander seems to have special appeal to suspended catfish.

On reservoirs in the south central states, channel catfish suspend in the thermocline during summer. They can be found in open water not related to any bottom structure. Because the fish are located in a narrow band, a graph recorder or flasher is needed to find the schools and their exact depths. Some fishermen catch these suspended cats on waterdogs fished from marker buoy rigs.

Trotline fishermen often use whole amphibians or parts of large frogs or toads for bait. These baits can also be fished with rod and reel, using egg sinker rigs (page 40) or Wolf River rigs (page 46).

How to Rig and Fish a Sliding Float

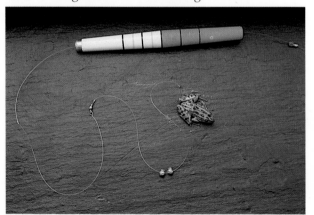

TIE a slip-bobber knot (page 70), then thread a bead and a 10-inch sliding float onto 20-pound mono. Add split-shot. Hook a frog through the hind leg or both lips with a 1/0 hook. Adjust the knot for the desired depth.

CAST the float into a deep eddy using a heavy-duty rod and reel. Allow the float to drift in a large circle, following the curl of the eddy. Good fishing usually begins in late evening and peaks at dawn.

LOCATE schools of suspended catfish with a graph recorder. This graph tape shows a dense band of catfish between 10 and 15 feet. The catfish remain at the same level regardless of the water depth.

How to Make and Fish a Marker Buoy Rig

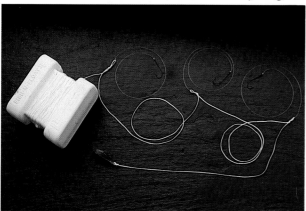

TIE 40 feet of heavy dacron line to a marker buoy or styrofoam float. Add a 2-ounce sinker. Using a tandem hook knot (page 39), attach two to four 20-pound mono leaders with 1/0 hooks. Space the leaders two feet apart.

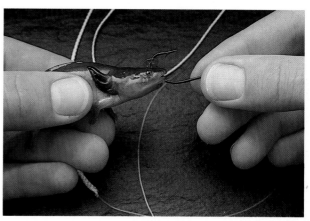

HOOK 4- to 6-inch waterdogs through both lips. Use bait-saver tabs to keep them on the hook. Some fishermen experiment with other baits, then switch to those that are producing the most fish.

ADJUST the depth to the level of the fish. Make a loop, twist it twice, then wrap it around the float. Make another loop and repeat. This simple variation of a half-hitch is easy to untie. Drop the markers upwind of the school.

CHECK the floats after they have drifted past the fish. If any appear to be bobbing or moving erratically, retrieve them and carefully pull in the catfish. Use a landing net to avoid losing the fish at boatside.

Northern Pike

A bass fishermen retrieving a salamander along the edge of a weedbed may be jolted by a vicious strike. He reels in the line, only to find it sheared off by the sharp teeth of a northern pike. Incidents like this are giving salamanders a reputation as an effective pike bait.

Waterdogs and spring lizards are proven pike baits. Other salamanders are still not widely used for northerns. But pike generally eat whatever they can find, so it is unlikely that they would strongly prefer one kind of salamander over another. A pike will grab any size salamander that swims near, but a 4- to 6-inch salamander works best for pike under 5 pounds. Anything larger is difficult to swallow. A northern over 10 pounds is more likely to strike an 8- to 9-inch salamander. Northern pike rarely take a dead bait. A rubber band rig will hold a salamander on the hook and keep it alive.

Frogs are a traditional pike bait in the North but are seldom used in other parts of the country.

NORTHERN PIKE may swallow a waterdog. Carry a longnose pliers to dislodge the hook. Use a steel leader to prevent the teeth from cutting the line.

How to Make and Fish a Rubber Band Rig

PUSH the head of a salamander through a #10 rubber band. Lodge the rubber band behind the gills and twist it once below the chin.

LOOP the rubber band back over the snout. Push a 2/0 hook through the lips, twist the rubber band again and loop it over the hook point.

ANCHOR the boat along a deep weedline. Lob-cast a slip-bobber rig toward the deep side of the weeds. Inch the bobber toward the boat.

Walleyes

Fishermen who specialize in catching trophy-class walleyes rank waterdogs as one of the top baits. Many lakes that grow big walleyes are packed with stunted perch, sunfish or other panfish. Catching walleyes in these lakes can be difficult because panfish constantly nip at worms, leeches, or minnows. But these small fish will not bother waterdogs.

Most anglers troll 4- to 5-inch waterdogs on slip-sinker rigs. Waterdogs 6 inches or longer may work better for big walleyes. Fishermen who use waterdogs are often frustrated by walleyes that bite short. The fish rip up the waterdog's tail but never touch the hook. To solve this problem, put a stinger hook in the tail (page 41) or rig the waterdog on a threaded harness (page 79).

The frog's popularity as a walleye bait has declined in recent years as more and more walleye fishermen switch to nightcrawlers and leeches. But some anglers still consider frogs a good bait, especially when walleyes move inshore in fall.

TROLL a waterdog through a school of walleyes. Make several passes over the school, because the fish may not strike immediately.

How to Fish a Super Hook Rig

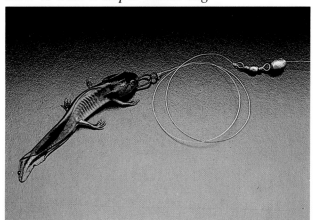

TIE a slip-sinker rig and add a #2 Super Hook. Spread the points, then pinch the hook on the waterdog just behind the gills. With this type of hook, the bait will stay alive indefinitely.

LOCATE walleyes with some type of depth finder. This video sonar unit shows a school of walleyes (arrow) along the edge of a drop-off. Toss out a marker buoy when you find the fish.

Crustaceans

Crustaceans

Young fish feed heavily on water fleas and other microscopic crustaceans. Many adult fish regularly eat crayfish and other larger crustaceans. This explains why crustaceans are effective as bait.

Crustaceans have external skeletons, or shells. To grow, they must shed their shells, or *molt*. Most crustaceans have several other features in common. They obtain oxygen either through gills or through the surface of their bodies, and they have antennae and jointed legs.

The following crustaceans are used for bait by freshwater fishermen:

CRAYFISH. Called *crawfish, crawdads* or *crabs,* these crustaceans are found in almost every type of fresh water, from large lakes and rivers to small creeks and sloughs. Young crayfish live around rocks or debris on bottom, but adults may inhabit open areas with little cover. Some types, called burrowing crayfish, live in damp soil.

GRASS SHRIMP. Some species of grass shrimp live in fresh water; others are found only in salt water. They are called *glass shrimp* because of their transparent appearance.

SCUDS. Common to many trout streams, scuds thrive in any cool, unpolluted water that is rich in oxygen and has ample rooted vegetation. They are sometimes called *sideswimmers* because they swim with their bodies turned sideways. These tiny crustaceans have been stocked in lakes as a supplement to natural trout foods.

MUD SHRIMP. This group includes *ghost shrimp* and *blue mud shrimp.* Although called shrimp, they are actually soft-bodied crabs that burrow into sand or mud flats of estuaries.

SALTWATER SHRIMP. These edible shrimp include pink, brown and white shrimp. Anglers most often use the young shrimp, which live in coastal estuaries before moving out to sea.

FRESHWATER SHRIMP. Sold as *river shrimp* along the lower Mississippi River, freshwater shrimp spawn in brackish waters. They range widely throughout large river systems, moving upsteam as far as the first major dam or obstruction. They often live in connecting lakes, channels or backwaters.

CRAYFISH are found throughout North America, except for much of the Rocky Mountain region. They are usually some shade of brown or green, but may be black, red, orange, or blue. Most are 2 to 4 inches long, not including claws. Crayfish have harder, thicker shells than other crustaceans. Males have larger claws than females. When approached, the crayfish propels itself backwards with quick flips of the tail.

GRASS SHRIMP are 1 to 2 inches long and have an almost glassy appearance. Saltwater types live in estuaries along the Atlantic and Gulf coasts. Freshwater species are most common in the southeastern United States.

SCUDS grow to ¾ inch in length and have thin, deep bodies. Scuds do not have a distinct tail. They live in fresh waters throughout the United States and Canada. Shown is a species of Gammarus.

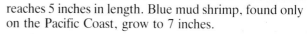

MUD SHRIMP inhabit tidal flats and beaches along the Pacific and Gulf coasts. Shown is the ghost shrimp, which reaches 5 inches in length. Blue mud shrimp, found only on the Pacific Coast, grow to 7 inches.

SALTWATER SHRIMP have short, tiny claws. They are commonly used for bait along the Atlantic and Gulf coasts. Anglers use the 3- to 5-inch young of pink, white and brown shrimp. Shown is a young brown shrimp.

FRESHWATER SHRIMP include several species found in the southern United States as far north as Illinois. They have long, narrow claws and long antennae. Freshwater shrimp range in size from 2 to 10 inches.

Catching Crustaceans

Catching crustaceans is easy if you understand their habits and use the proper tools. Most crustaceans avoid bright sunlight. They feed and move about mostly after dark. Traps catch more crustaceans at night than at any other time.

The simplest way to catch a few crayfish is to grab them after turning over rocks in shallow water. To catch larger numbers of crayfish, use an umbrella net, seine or trap. Most fishermen believe that wooden traps work better than metal traps. Bait the trap with any type of unspoiled meat. Chop or mince the bait so it gives off a strong odor.

In lakes, crayfish are most often trapped along rocky shorelines, under bridges or on deep rock piles. In streams, look for them in rocky areas where the current is not too strong. If there is no bottom cover, search in the shade of overhanging banks.

Hand nets or fine-mesh seines work well for catching grass shrimp. In saltwater estuaries, look for them in shallow grass beds. In freshwater lakes, they can be found in dense mats of floating vegetation near shore and in submerged weeds such as coontail, hydrilla and eelgrass.

Scuds also hide in vegetation. The largest species inhabit clear, cool streams and spring-fed ponds, usually in water less than 3 feet deep. Most fishermen catch them with fine-mesh dip nets or cheesecloth seines. In many waters, they are too small to be used as bait.

Anglers gather mud shrimp in estuaries throughout the year. Look for them in sand or mud flats exposed by low tides. Flats near river mouths usually hold the largest numbers. Many fishermen use clam tubes and shrimp guns (page 131) to collect them.

Pink, brown and white shrimp breed at sea. The newly-hatched shrimp move into estuaries in late winter or spring. In about two months, the young reach bait size. They are caught with push nets (page 130) or seines on shallow, muddy, grass flats. By mid-summer, the 3- to 5-inch shrimp begin moving back to sea. Shrimp movement increases with windy weather, heavy outgoing tides, or sudden cold snaps that lower the water temperature. Migrations generally taper off by November and end sometime in December.

Migrating shrimp can be easily caught with dip nets, cast nets (page 29) and shrimp traps (page 131). Look for them where tidal currents sweep past docks or piers, or where the shrimp funnel through narrow channels on their way back to the ocean.

Freshwater shrimp are found in estuaries and in large rivers, including connecting bays and lakes. In spring, they can be trapped near power plants where they move into warm-water discharges. In summer, bait-size shrimp are caught with *willow sets* (page 131) along muddy streambanks. They can also be trapped in river channels, sometimes in water as deep as 25 feet. In winter, freshwater shrimp are inactive.

How to Catch Crayfish

CRAYFISH TRAPS are set on rock piles as deep as 20 feet. Bait with fresh, cut fish in a mesh bag. Place the bag so crayfish must enter the trap to reach the bait.

POLE-MOUNTED CANS are used to catch crayfish. Use a stick to chase the crayfish backwards into the can. Lift quickly; water will drain through holes.

MUD CHIMNEYS are the entrances to crayfish burrows. They are found along lakeshores, streambanks and pond edges. Crayfish sometimes leave their burrows during rainy weather or at night, and can be found nearby.

MINNOW TRAPS catch crayfish in shallow, rocky areas. Expand the entrance slightly and bait with a punctured can of cat food. Remove crayfish daily.

UMBRELLA NETS can be used in shallow water. Bait with chicken necks. Lift the trap after dark or in early morning, using a stiff pole with a hook on the end.

How to Seine Shrimp and Crayfish

SEINE saltwater shrimp in estuaries. Look for grass beds on shallow tidal flats. To catch grass shrimp, pull a fine-mesh seine through sparse vegetation near the shore of a lake or estuary. For crayfish, stretch the seine across a stream, while another person turns over rocks upstream and chases crayfish into the net.

How to Catch Grass Shrimp

DIP weeds with a hand net. Dump them into a floating screen box. The plants float, but the shrimp swim to the bottom of the box. Shake the weeds, remove them and transfer the shrimp to a bucket of water.

ROLL a push net through a grass bed. The net has a flat lower edge that scrapes along bottom. A roller just behind the leading edge makes pushing easier. The nets are usually 1½ to 3 feet wide, but can be made in any size.

How to Catch Scuds

GRAB several handfuls of fine-leaved aquatic plants from the shallows of a cold stream or pond. Submerge the vegetation in a pail of water and shake it vigorously to dislodge scuds.

COLLECT scuds from fine gravel or from beds of water-cress or other vegetation in clear, cold-water streams. Use a screened pitchfork (page 86) to scoop up clumps of vegetation or to sift scuds from the gravel.

How to Catch Mud Shrimp With a Clam Tube

COLLECT mud shrimp at low tide. Look for the 1-inch burrows on tidal flats. Use a clam tube or shrimp gun.

PUSH a clam tube down over a burrow. Cover the air hole at the top of the tube, then pull up steadily.

DUMP the mud or sand from the tube to find shrimp. In a short time you can find enough shrimp for a day's fishing.

How to Make and Use a Shrimp Gun for Mud Shrimp

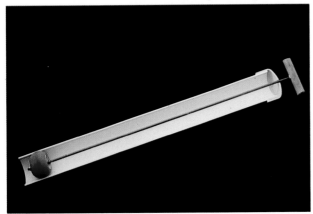

MAKE a shrimp gun (cross section) from 30 inches of 3-inch PVC pipe. Attach an end cap with a hole for a 3-foot, ¼-inch steel rod with threaded ends. Use nuts and washers to compress a 3-inch rubber ball. Add a handle.

PLACE the gun over a burrow. Pull up the plunger quickly to draw in sand, water and shrimp. Push the plunger to expel the contents. Put the shrimp in water. Shrimp guns work best in sand but can be used in mud.

How to Catch Saltwater and Freshwater Shrimp

DIP NETS catch saltwater shrimp around docks, piers or bridges. Shine a powerful light into the water. Their eyes will reflect the light.

SHRIMP TRAPS set in channels catch saltwater shrimp moving with the current. Shrimp enter the rectangular openings and cannot escape.

WILLOW SETS attract freshwater shrimp. Shove the willows into a muddy riverbank. After several days shake the branches over a catch box.

131

Keeping Crustaceans

KEEP enough shrimp for a day's fishing in a large cooler. Cover the bottom with ice, then add a thick layer of weeds. Scatter the shrimp, then add more plants.

Keeping crustaceans alive requires many of the same techniques used for baitfish (page 33). Like fish, crustaceans have gills and will use up oxygen in the water. Use flow-through buckets or styrofoam containers that allow oxygen to pass through the sides. Crustaceans stay alive longer in cool water than in warm water. However, temperatures below 50°F will kill saltwater shrimp.

Unlike fish, crustaceans can obtain oxygen from air, but only if their gills are wet. Some bait shop operators keep crayfish in tanks where water splashes in and drains out. To keep crayfish alive during a fishing trip, pack them in damp weeds or moss.

After a crayfish molts, its body is extremely soft, but starts to harden immediately. Within a day or two, the shell hardens completely. Many fishermen prefer soft-shelled crayfish. To keep the shells soft, pack crayfish in damp newspaper, weeds or moss, and refrigerate at about 40°F. This delays the hardening process for as long as 10 to 12 days.

Freshwater, saltwater and mud shrimp will also stay alive in damp weeds. Saltwater and mud shrimp live longer if packed in seaweed. Mud shrimp can also be kept in a bucket or milk carton with an inch of water. They have soft, delicate bodies and must be handled gently. Place dead mud shrimp on ice immediately. Fishermen prefer fresh mud shrimp. Once thawed, frozen mud shrimp become too soft to keep on the hook.

Grass shrimp can be kept in water, but if they die, the water softens their bodies rapidly. Some fishermen prefer to keep them cool and dry. Then, if the shrimp die, the bodies remain firm.

Crayfish and saltwater shrimp can be frozen and, when thawed, the meat will still be firm. Freeze only fresh crustaceans because their flesh softens rapidly after death. Turn down the temperature of your freezer so they freeze quickly. You can save space by freezing only the tails of crayfish.

To preserve grass shrimp and scuds, dry them on newspaper in the sun. When the shells feel hard, freeze the crustaceans in plastic bags.

GRASS SHRIMP kept cool and dry will stay alive for several hours. Place ice in the bottom of a styrofoam bucket, cover with dry newspaper, then add shrimp.

CRAYFISH should be refrigerated to be kept alive for an extended period. In a styrofoam cooler, alternate layers of wet newspapers and crayfish.

SHRIMP can be kept for long periods in a submerged live box. Fine mesh is needed for grass shrimp. Lower the box to the bottom or under a dock to avoid strong light.

SCUDS require cool, fresh water. Use an insulated container in warm weather. For long-term storage, aerate the water with an aquarium pump.

FREEZE scuds to insure a year-round supply. Drop several into each section of an ice cube tray and add water. Keep the cubes frozen in plastic bags.

Fishing With Crustaceans

Fishing experts agree that crustaceans appeal to fish because of scent. A chunk of shrimp meat tossed into a flowing channel has an almost magical power to attract saltwater fish. Within minutes, fish detect the scent and appear out of nowhere. The scent of crustaceans also appeals to freshwater fish.

Anglers in coastal areas have found that the shrimp used for catching saltwater fish work almost as well for some types of freshwater fish. Along the Atlantic and Gulf coasts, shrimp account for many largemouth bass in estuaries and other brackish waters. Panfish and catfish anglers in waters farther inland also use fresh shrimp meat.

Other crustaceans such as grass shrimp, scuds and mud shrimp are becoming more popular in certain parts of the United States and Canada. But with the exception of crayfish, crustaceans have not gained nationwide popularity.

Crayfish work best for smallmouth bass. But they will catch almost any large gamefish including catfish, steelhead, and other large trout. Small crayfish are used for crappies, perch, rock bass, shellcrackers, longear sunfish and other panfish. Peeled crayfish tails also make good panfish bait.

Many anglers believe that soft-shelled crayfish are more effective than those with hard shells. Some fishermen are convinced that gamefish will not strike a crayfish with large claws. So they remove the claws before fishing or select only the smaller-clawed females.

Grass shrimp are popular for sunfish and crappies in some southeastern states. They are seldom used in other areas, even though they are found south of a line from Maine to Texas.

Scuds, though only ½ inch long, have a scent that is strong enough to attract panfish and trout. Fishermen must use tiny, light-wire hooks because of the scud's small size and fragile body. Be careful when casting because they are easily torn from the hook.

Mud shrimp are used in coastal rivers of the Pacific Northwest for steelhead, salmon, sturgeon and smallmouth bass. Mud shrimp are so effective for salmon and steelhead that efforts have been made to ban them on some Canadian rivers.

Freshwater shrimp have become popular with some catfish and bass fishermen in the lower Mississippi and Ohio river basins. The 2- to 3-inch sizes make the best bait. They are not widely used elsewhere.

Crustaceans are harder to use than most natural baits. To be effective, they require special hooking and rigging techniques. Most have soft flesh, so they tear off the hook easily when cast or trolled. As a result, they must be hooked through the tough parts of the shell, threaded, or hooked with rubber band rigs. Some anglers wrap crustaceans on the hook with pipe cleaners or soft copper wire. Peeled crayfish tails can be firmed up by boiling.

Hooking a fish can be difficult when using large crustaceans. Some fishermen cut shrimp into small pieces to keep fish from stealing the bait. When fish are striking short on whole crayfish, try using only the tails. When fish refuse to swallow a hard-shelled crayfish, try a soft-shell. If fish can crush the shell, more of the hook becomes exposed.

Smallmouth Bass

When fishermen think of crayfish, they think of smallmouth bass. Biologists studying smallmouth diets usually find that crayfish are the most common food item. The reason is that smallmouths and crayfish often share the same rocky bottoms. Fishing in the rocks requires some special techniques. Many anglers use a snag-resistant sinker such as a bottom-walker. With this type of sinker, you can retrieve a crayfish along bottom without snagging constantly.

Another popular technique is freelining. Cast an unweighted crayfish into a rocky area. Let it sink, then inch it slowly along bottom. Keep a little tension on the line at all times. If given slack, the crayfish will crawl under a rock.

Smallmouth anglers hook crayfish through the tail for most types of fishing. When using a bobber, hook the crayfish through the top of the shell. Bobber-fishing works well when smallmouths are located over rock piles that are too snaggy for casting or trolling. Adjust the bobber so the crayfish hangs just a few inches off bottom.

Popular Crayfish Rigs

SPLIT-SHOT RIGS are tied with a #2 or #4 hook on 8-pound line. Hook a crayfish through the tail. Pinch on enough split-shot to sink the bait to bottom.

BOTTOM-WALKER RIGS are made by tying a 24-inch leader to the top eye. Hook a crayfish on a #2 or #4 hook. Tie the line to the other eye.

Largemouth Bass

The weedy, muddy bottoms frequented by largemouth bass hardly seem the place to use crayfish as bait. But crayfish work almost as well for largemouth bass as they do for smallmouths.

Fishermen use many of the same crayfish rigs and techniques for both species. To keep crayfish from disappearing in the soft mud, anglers suspend them from a bobber or attach a small float just ahead of the hook. Another effective technique is hooking a crayfish in the tail with a large floating jig head.

Along the southern Atlantic and Gulf coasts, bass fishermen have discovered that live saltwater shrimp make excellent bait for largemouths. Bass in cypress swamps and other brackish waters feed heavily on the young shrimp. To keep shrimp alive as long as possible, hook them in the head, just in front of the dark spot on the back. Some anglers pinch split-shot above the hook and cast with light tackle. Others use cane poles to drop shrimp into heavy cover or places that could not be reached by casting.

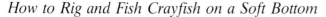

How to Rig and Fish Crayfish on a Soft Bottom

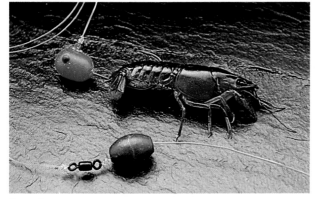

THREAD a ¼-ounce egg sinker on 10-pound mono and attach a swivel. Add a 3-foot leader of 8-pound mono and a large floating jig. Hook the crayfish through the tail.

RETRIEVE the crayfish slowly. The floating jig will keep the bait above the silt. Retrieving too fast pulls the crayfish to the bottom.

Sunfish

Sunfish anglers who had spent years fishing with worms and insects were startled to learn the results of a study conducted in one southern state. Fishermen tested a variety of baits to determine which were most effective for catching bluegills. Of all the natural baits tested, live grass shrimp caught the most bluegills per hour of fishing. The shrimp

caught bluegills at nearly twice the rate of crickets and more than twice the rate of worms.

Grass shrimp are not available in most areas of the country, but anglers have some alternatives. Scuds, though not as large as grass shrimp, have a similar scent. Some anglers mash up scuds and rub the fluid on plastic jigs and other artificial lures. Or, they hook on a whole scud, which gives off enough scent to attract fish.

Dead crustaceans work as well as live ones. Some fishermen buy frozen shrimp at a grocery store, then cut them into small pieces for sunfish bait. Juices from the meat draw sunfish. Many anglers believe that the strong scent makes frozen shrimp more attractive to fish than fresh shrimp. If shrimp are not available, substitute cut-up crayfish tails.

How to Fish With Scuds

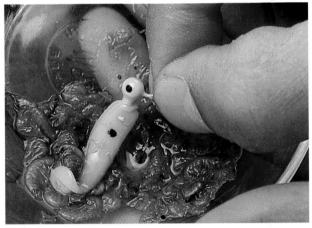

MASH scuds in a small cup. Rub the juices on a 1/16- or 1/32-ounce plastic jig. The soft plastic absorbs scent better than most other materials.

TIP a teardrop jig with one or more scuds. Add a split-shot and small bobber. Cast gently to avoid tearing the bait off the hook.

How to Rig and Fish Shrimp Meat

CUT off the head and tail and slice the body into 3/8-inch chunks. Some anglers peel the shell.

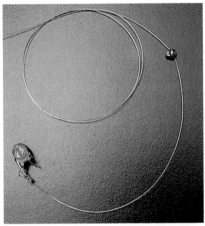

TIE a #8 hook to 4-pound mono. Pinch on split-shot 8 inches above the hook. Thread on the meat.

CHUM the area with leftover shrimp parts. The scent draws sunfish. Keep the bait close to bottom.

How to Fish With Grass Shrimp

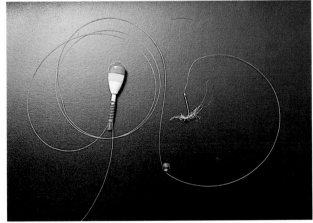

TIE a #6 or #8 hook on 4-pound mono. Attach a small bobber. Split-shot is optional. Thread on a grass shrimp or hook it through the back.

DROP the bait into pockets in submerged weeds. Jiggle it, then let it rest a few seconds. If nothing bites, lift the bait and move it to another pocket.

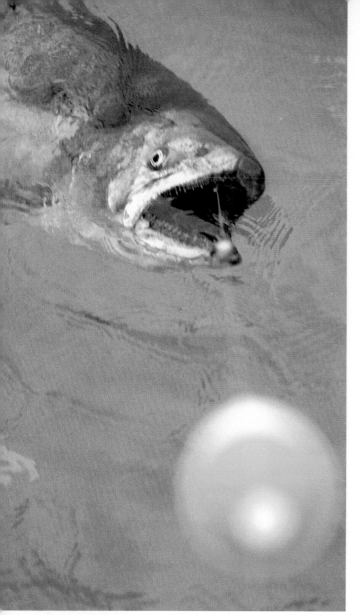

LARGE FLOATS keep the mud shrimp just bumping bottom. If allowed to drag, the shrimp will catch on rocks and soon tear off the hook.

Salmon & Steelhead

Fishermen seldom think of crustaceans as bait for salmon or steelhead. But the flaming orange flesh of many trout and salmon is proof that these fish feed heavily on crustaceans. The orange coloration comes from *carotene*, a pigment in the shells and flesh of crustaceans. It is the same pigment that makes a lobster turn red when boiled.

Anglers in the Pacific Northwest know that salmon and steelhead have a taste for crustaceans. Ghost and blue mud shrimp have become popular baits in coastal rivers. At times, they are more effective than fresh spawn.

Mud shrimp can be drift-fished, but they will not stay on the hook as long as a spawn bag. To keep the bait on the hook longer, some fishermen on slow rivers rig the mud shrimp with a large float so the bait does not drag on bottom. Other anglers snell on a rubber band to help hold the shrimp on the hook.

When fishing from boats in a popular pool or run, Pacific Coast fishermen often anchor in a row, called a *hogline*. They fasten the anchor rope to the boat with a quick-release clip. When a fish bites, the angler unclips the anchor rope so the boat drifts downstream, away from the lines of other fishermen. A float attached to the anchor line enables the angler to return to the same position after playing and landing the fish.

How to Rig and Fish a Mud Shrimp

SLIDE a 1- to 3-ounce egg sinker onto 15-pound mono and tie on a swivel. Add a 24-inch leader of 10-pound mono, then snell on a 1/0 plastic-worm hook and a #8 rubber band. Thread the center part of the shrimp onto the hook and pull the rubber band over the tail.

ANCHOR the boat in a hogline, then cast the mud shrimp straight downstream. Reel in slack. Set the hook at the first sign of a bite. Keep the drag adjusted properly because a big steelhead or salmon heading downstream in fast current can easily snap the line.

Stream Trout

Fly fishermen who check the stomachs of trout often find them packed with scuds. Stream fishermen tie flies to resemble these tiny, shrimp-like crustaceans. But anglers rarely use real scuds because they are difficult to keep on a hook. In lakes, however, scuds can be fished with a casting bubble filled with water.

Crayfish are seldom used in small creeks but are an effective bait on larger streams, especially for big brown trout. For smaller trout, some anglers use crayfish tails.

How to Rig and Use Scuds

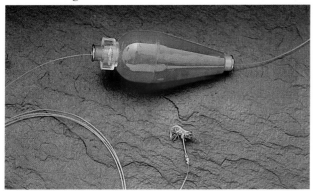

SLIDE a casting bubble onto 4-pound mono. Fill with water. Twist the top to secure it 4 feet up the line. Thread one to three scuds on a #12 or #14 light-wire hook.

LOB the rig and retrieve slowly. Most anglers use clear casting bubbles, but some believe that red or orange bubbles attract more fish.

How to Rig Crayfish With a Rubber Band

WRAP a #8 or #10 rubber band around the body of a crayfish no more than 2 inches long. Slip a #4 or #6 hook under the rubber band. Attach split-shot about 2 feet up the line. Some anglers find it easier to set the hook when all of it is exposed.

CAST the crayfish into a shaded area of the stream. Lob the bait gently to avoid tearing it off the hook. Let the current bounce the bait along bottom. Or cast the crayfish into a riffle and keep a tight line as the current washes the bait downstream into the pool.

Other Natural Baits

Fishermen discover many new baits by checking the stomachs of fish. In addition to a wide array of minnows and insects, anglers sometimes find turtles, mice, lizards, snails, ducklings or other types of baby birds.

Imaginative anglers use many of these baits, plus a few that are even more unusual, such as baby alligators and small snakes. Fishermen in the South know that garter, DeKay's and various kinds of water snakes are ideal baits for largemouth bass. The snakes swim enticingly and are among the liveliest natural baits.

Muskie fishermen in the North occasionally hook on gophers, mice and other small mammals, then let them swim over known muskie haunts. Even a well-fed muskie is not likely to ignore such an easy meal. Largemouth bass fishermen also use mice for bait.

Snails and slugs are used to catch panfish. Slugs can be collected from a garden and snails from a weedy lakeshore or damp woodland. Some fishermen hook on the entire snail; others crack the shell and use only the body as bait.

These unusual baits, though effective, are used by relatively few fishermen. Other baits, including salmon eggs, clams, cut-baits and fish parts, are more popular. These baits are discussed on the following pages. Also included is information on dried, freeze-dried and bottled baits, along with tips for curing, freezing and bottling your own bait.

Salmon Eggs

When steelhead or salmon move into spawning streams, salmon eggs catch more fish than any other bait. Eggs from any large trout work equally well. Lure manufacturers are aware of the effectiveness of salmon eggs. They make a variety of lures that resemble the shape or color of eggs. These imitations include cork and sponge balls, single rubber eggs, yarn, and dozens of spoons and plugs.

Egg imitations do not work as well as the real thing. When a fish picks up an artificial egg, it quickly rejects it. With real eggs, the fish is likely to mouth the bait an instant longer, giving the fisherman more time to set the hook. Also, natural eggs are more effective because they *milk*, or emit a whitish substance with a scent that attracts trout and salmon.

Some anglers prefer a single egg on a short-shank egg hook. Others remove an egg sac, called a *skein*, from a female salmon or trout, then cut the sac into chunks, each about ¾ inch square. The delicate sac

covering and connective tissue hold the eggs on the hook. As spawning time approaches, the eggs become larger and looser within the skein and more difficult to keep on the hook. Then fishermen tie the eggs in bags made of fine nylon mesh. Eggs tied in spawn bags hold together much better and stay on the hook longer.

In areas where steelhead or salmon fishing is popular, bait shops may carry fresh eggs or spawn bags. If spawn is not available, check a fish-cleaning facility or ask a successful fisherman for a small chunk of spawn. After catching your first female fish, you will have a good supply.

Fresh salmon eggs look clear and are almost fluorescent. After a few days they take on a milky appearance and become mushy. Salmon eggs can be preserved for future fishing trips. Keep the eggs cool and dry, and preserve them (page 146) within two or three days.

How to Gather Salmon Eggs

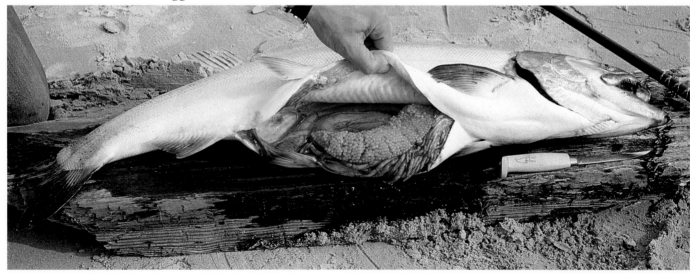

OPEN the belly by making a shallow cut through the skin. The two egg sacs, or skeins, run the length of the cavity and are connected to the body on both ends. Try not to damage the fragile tissue covering the skeins.

GRASP one skein and pull gently to break it free from the cavity. Then remove the other skein.

LAY the skeins on a bed of ice for a day's fishing. To keep them longer, place in unsealed plastic bags on ice.

How to Cure Single Eggs

RINSE large eggs in a strainer using cold water. Allow them to drain for one to two hours. As the eggs dry, the shells collapse, giving them a wrinkled appearance.

DISSOLVE 1 tablespoon boric acid crystals per quart of water. Add the dried eggs; stir occasionally. Eggs absorb the solution and lose their wrinkles within one hour.

How to Prepare Chunked Spawn

WRAP individual skeins in paper towels. They should be well-drained and free of excess blood. Refrigerate for two to three days to remove any remaining moisture.

CUT off ¾-inch square pieces, each with skein membrane attached. Drop the egg chunks into powdered, non-detergent borax.

How to Tie a Spawn Bag

PLACE a small chunk of spawn or several large, single eggs on a 2- to 3-inch square of red or white nylon mesh. A piece of nylon stocking will also work.

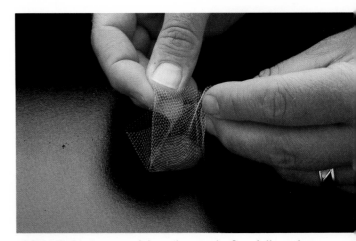

PICK UP the corners of the nylon mesh. Carefully gather them in one hand to form a spawn bag from ⅜ to ⅝ inch in diameter.

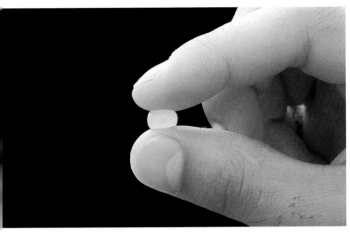

SQUEEZE an egg lightly to make sure it feels firm and rubbery. If the egg pops, it has not soaked up enough boric acid solution.

DRAIN the preserved eggs, then spoon them into baby food jars or other small, airtight containers. If refrigerated, the eggs will last up to six months.

ROLL the pieces in borax until coated. Borax preserves the eggs but washes off quickly when the bait is dropped into the water.

DROP chunks into a jar with a 1-inch layer of borax. Cover with an airtight lid. Shake to coat pieces again. Refrigerate in the jar for up to two weeks or freeze.

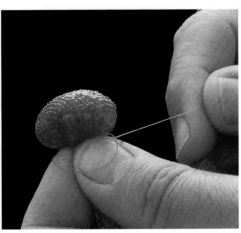

WRAP five loops of the thread around the gathered mesh. Make sure the bag is formed tightly around the eggs.

PINCH the loops so they will not unravel. Tie a series of half-hitches to secure the bag.

TRIM excess materials. Drop the bags into borax and shake the jar. Refrigerate up to two weeks or freeze.

Fishing With Salmon Eggs

Drift-fishing with spawn for steelhead or salmon is one of the most difficult techniques to master. At first glance, it seems simple. Just make a short cast quartering upstream, then let the bait drift downstream at the same speed as the current. But the technique requires a sensitive touch because every pebble in the stream bottom feels like the gentle nudge of a steelhead or salmon picking up the bait. To detect these subtle bites, use a long graphite fly rod and monofilament line. This combination provides maximum feel.

Drift-fishing requires a great deal of patience. Steelhead or salmon may ignore a bait drifted past them dozens of times, then suddenly decide to strike.

The type of water determines whether to use a single egg, a chunk of eggs or a spawn bag. On streams, drift-fishermen use spawn bags because repeated casting would tear spawn chunks off the hook. When streams are high and muddy, snell colored yarn on the hook as an attractor. A spawn chunk is sometimes better when still-fishing in a quiet pool or in slack water near a stream mouth. In low, clear water, a short-shank hook buried in a single egg may work better than a spawn chunk. Some fishermen chum with a handful of eggs, then toss out a single egg suspended from a bobber.

When using salmon eggs, it pays to change bait frequently. When the eggs become pale and washed-out, replace them with fresh ones.

How to Hook Salmon Eggs

SINGLE EGGS are hooked by (1) piercing one edge, (2) sliding the egg up the shaft, (3) turning it and pushing it back down to bury the point.

SPAWN CHUNKS are held with an egg loop. Snell a hook (page 79). Lay a chunk in the loop along the shaft. Pierce the membrane with the hook.

SPAWN BAGS should be placed on a short-shank hook so only the eye and tip of the point are exposed. Fluorescent yarn is optional.

How to Fish a Single Egg or Spawn Chunk

TIE a slip-sinker rig, then bury an egg hook in a fresh or preserved salmon egg. Hook size depends on the diameter of the egg. Some anglers prefer a chunk of spawn held on a #4 hook by an egg loop.

WADE into the water to reach fish beyond casting distance from shore. Using a surf-casting rod, cast the bait and leave the bail open as you walk back to shore. Tighten the line, prop up the rod and wait for a bite.

How to Drift-fish a Spawn Bag

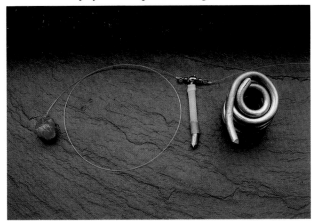

TIE a drift-fishing rig by attaching the line and an 8- to 12-pound leader to a surgical tubing sinker. Insert a piece of lead wire into the tube, then add a spawn bag. When snagged, the lead pulls out and frees the rig.

DROP the bait vertically into small pockets that cannot be drift-fished. Steelhead and salmon will often rest in eddies and other slack water areas during their migrations upstream.

CAST across current and slightly upstream. Keep the rod tip high and the line taut as the bait drifts. The sinker should tick bottom as it moves along but should not drag. Set the hook immediately when the bait stops.

Clams

A school of sunfish will quickly tear apart an open clam dropped into the water. Many fish crush and eat small clams as part of their diet. Larger clams are protected by thick shells, but their meat makes good bait. In addition to sunfish, clam meat works well for catfish, sturgeon, drum and other river species.

Big rivers support the largest clam populations. Clams feed by siphoning particles from the water, so the biggest clams live where the current sweeps food to them. In rivers and large lakes, they are generally found in 8 to 20 feet of water. In smaller lakes and streams, they inhabit 1- to 6-foot depths. Clams prefer mud, sand or fine-gravel bottoms.

Gather clams by hand in clear, shallow water. Their tracks can be seen easily on sand bottoms. In deeper or turbid water, feel for clams with your bare feet or dive to collect them.

Most fish prefer fresh clam meat, but catfish are attracted to clams that are slightly spoiled. Soak the meat in sour milk for several days to give it a rubbery texture and strong scent.

The soft texture of clam meat makes it difficult to keep on a hook. For casting, put the meat inside a mesh bag similar to a spawn bag (page 146). Some fishermen use a bait loop to rig clam meat. Gently lob the bait, or use a cane pole and carefully lower the clam meat into the water. Anglers who bottom-fish for catfish often attach a small float just ahead of the hook. This keeps the clam meat several inches above bottom.

KEEP clams alive as long as one or two days in a bucket of water out of the sun. They will live for weeks in a submerged live box.

How to Rig and Fish Clams for Catfish

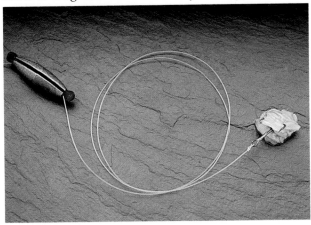

TIE a #4 treble hook on 20-pound line. Attach a 1- to 2-ounce sinker 2 feet above the hook. Form the meat around the hook, piercing it with all points. Some anglers wrap the soft meat on a bait-holder treble hook.

LOWER the clam meat into a likely catfish spot using a 12-foot cane pole. Some fishermen set several poles along a slow-moving stretch of river, pushing the ends deep into the mud bank.

WAIT for a catfish to grab the bait. The strong scent of the milk-soured meat will draw catfish, especially channels and blues. Rubbery meat will stay on the hook longer than fresh meat.

How to Rig Clams for Sunfish

FEEL the meat to locate the firm muscle (arrow). Scrape out the clam, then cut off the tough portion.

THREAD the firm meat on a #6 or #8 long-shank hook. Cut the softer meat into small pieces for chum.

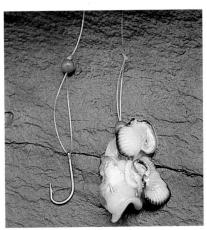

RIG a bait loop by sliding on a bead and hook. Thread the line through the bead again. Tie a knot to secure it.

Cut-baits & Fish Parts

Most freshwater gamefish prefer a live baitfish to a piece of fish flesh. But there are times when chunks of fish work equally well or better. Following ice-out, fishermen catch lake trout on strips of sucker meat still-fished on bottom. When striped bass congregate below power dams on their spring spawning runs, anglers use baitfish sliced crosswise into chunks or cut in half.

Fishermen cut the heads off baitfish, then troll or drift the plug-cut bodies. Properly prepared and rigged, a plug-cut fish has a wide, rolling action. Combined with smell, this makes the bait more attractive than a whole baitfish or artificial lure. Plug-cut baitfish are used to catch salmon, trout and striped bass.

Oily fish such as smelt, alewives, anchovies, shad and herring usually make the best cut-baits. Their scent is evidently more attractive to gamefish than the scent of lean-fleshed fish.

Other fish parts can be effective. Panfish anglers know that a throat latch cut from a small fish will often catch as many white bass, crappies, yellow perch or rock bass as a live minnow. And, a fisherman can often catch several fish on the same throat latch. Some anglers use an eyeball from a dead fish to tip a jig or other artificial lure.

How to Cut and Hook a Throat Latch

REMOVE the throat latch from a small panfish with a sharp knife. Some fishermen prefer to leave the pelvic fins attached for extra action.

HOOK the throat latch through the tip. Use a short-shank #6 hook on a split-shot rig, or tip an ⅛-ounce jig with the piece of flesh.

How to Prepare and Rig a Plug-cut Baitfish

SLICE off the head so the cut edge is slanted from top to bottom and from side to side. Remove the guts. Cut this way, the bait will roll when pulled through the water.

INSERT the rear hook of a mooching rig (page 49) under the skin above the vent. Bring the point back out, then pull the hook toward the tail until only the eye remains under the skin.

PUSH the front hook into the body cavity and out the back. The hook should pierce the backbone to hold the baitfish securely. The line connecting the hooks should not be tight.

How to Prepare and Rig Other Cut Baitfish

FILLET a sucker, leaving the skin attached. Cut it into 1 × 2-inch strips and butterfly the ends, if desired. Push a #2 hook through the skin at one end. Still-fish on bottom for lake trout or use the meat to tip a jig.

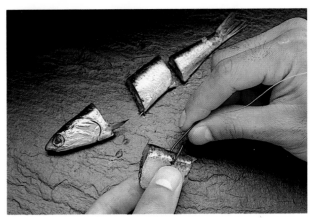

SLICE an anchovy, shad or other oily baitfish into 1-inch chunks. Push a 1/0 to 3/0 hook through the back, piercing the skin on both sides. Bottom-fish in tailraces to catch striped bass or catfish.

Preserved Baits

Fishermen can buy almost every type of natural bait in preserved form. Nightcrawlers, leeches, baitfish, crayfish, fish eggs and even insects are bottled, wet-packed, dried or freeze-dried.

Bottled and wet-packed baits are preserved in formaldehyde. Dried baits are soaked in a preservative, air-dried and then packaged. Freeze-dried baits are processed under high pressure at sub-zero temperatures. They turn out drier and lighter than air-dried baits and must be soaked until soft and pliable before they are used.

To restore freeze-dried baits to their original condition, add water to the package or soak the baits individually. Soaking time averages 20 to 30 minutes but may be several hours for large baitfish or frogs. Warm water shortens the softening time. To restore a bait faster, inject it with water by using a worm blower (page 70) or syringe.

Preserved baits rarely work as well as live ones. But in areas where live bait is not available or is illegal to use, preserved baits are a good second choice. Dried and freeze-dried baits come in handy on fishing trips to remote wilderness areas. Steelhead and salmon fishermen sometimes use bottled salmon eggs or spawn bags to catch their first female fish, then switch to fresh spawn. Ice fishermen catch panfish by tipping teardrop jigs with freeze-dried insect larvae, such as waxworms.

Other fishermen keep preserved baits handy just in case they run out of live bait. A package of dried shiners or a bottle of salmon eggs will keep for years in a tackle box.

How to Cure Baitfish

CURE baitfish in a mixture of equal parts of salt and sugar. Keep them in ice cream buckets or other plastic or glass containers.

FORM a single layer of fish on a ½-inch bed of the salt-sugar mixture. Make sure the fish do not touch each other or the salt will not penetrate.

ADD several more layers of salt and baitfish. The bait will be preserved after 48 hours at room temperature. Refrigerate the fish in plastic bags.

154

How to Freeze or Bottle Baits

FREEZE baitfish for long-term storage. Separate them on a cookie sheet to keep them from freezing together in a chunk. Once the fish are frozen, package them in freezer bags, each with a day's supply.

BOTTLE minnows or other baits in a small jar. Pour isopropyl alcohol to within ½ inch of the top. Add two drops of anise oil to eliminate the smell of the alcohol. Add more alcohol to top off the jar. Cap tightly.

Index

156

Cy DeCosse Incorporated offers Hunting
& Fishing Products at special subscriber
discounts. For information write:

Hunting & Fishing Products
5900 Green Oak Drive
Minnetonka, MN 55343